CEMETERY TOURS
AND PROGRAMMING

About the Series

The American Association for State and Local History Book Series addresses issues critical to the field of state and local history through interpretive, intellectual, scholarly, and educational texts. To submit a proposal or manuscript to the series, please request proposal guidelines from AASLH headquarters: AASLH Editorial Board, 1717 Church St., Nashville, Tennessee 37203. Telephone: (615) 320-3203. Website: www.aaslh.org.

About the Organization

The American Association for State and Local History (AASLH) is a national history membership association headquartered in Nashville, Tennessee. AASLH provides leadership and support for its members who preserve and interpret state and local history in order to make the past more meaningful to all Americans. AASLH members are leaders in preserving, researching, and interpreting traces of the American past to connect the people, thoughts, and events of yesterday with the creative memories and abiding concerns of people, communities, and our nation today. In addition to sponsorship of this book series, AASLH publishes *History News* magazine, a newsletter, technical leaflets and reports, and other materials; confers prizes and awards in recognition of outstanding achievement in the field; supports a broad education program and other activities designed to help members work more effectively; and advocates on behalf of the discipline of history. To join AASLH, go to www.aaslh.org or contact Membership Services, AASLH, 1717 Church St., Nashville, TN 37203.

CEMETERY TOURS AND PROGRAMMING

A Guide

RACHEL WOLGEMUTH

ROWMAN & LITTLEFIELD
Lanham • Boulder • New York • London

Published by Rowman & Littlefield
A wholly owned subsidary of The Rowman & Littlefield Publishing Group, Inc.
4501 Forbes Boulevard, Suite 200, Lanham, Maryland 20706
www.rowman.com

Unit A, Whitacre Mews, 26-34 Stannary Street, London SE11 4AB

British Library Cataloguing in Publication Information Available

Library of Congress Cataloging-in-Publication Data

Names: Wolgemuth, Rachel, author.
Title: Cemetery tours and programming : a guide / Rachel Wolgemuth.
Description: Lanham, Maryland : Rowman & Littlefield, 2016. | Series:
   American Association for State and Local History book series | Includes
   bibliographical references and index.
Identifiers: LCCN 2015042900| ISBN 9781442263178 (cloth : alk. paper) | ISBN
   9781442263185 (pbk. : alk. paper) | ISBN 9781442263192 (electronic)
Subjects: LCSH: Cemeteries--Management. | Cemeteries--Recreational use.
Classification: LCC GT3320 .W65 2016 | DDC 363.7/5068--dc23 LC record available
   at http://lccn.loc.gov/2015042900

Printed in the United States of America

CONTENTS

Foreword

What is past is prologue. And what is the American cemetery but a window to our past and, indeed, a prologue to our worldly fate? That which tethers us to history softly communicates our future and, in doing so, may offer no better reason than to revel in the here and now. The American cemetery is a lesson on living just waiting to be learned. I can think of no better place to begin than within the pages of this text.

Perhaps you are reading this as a cemetery employee or volunteer seeking methods to commence or expand the programming of your site. Perhaps you are a community member interested in becoming involved in your own local cemetery. Perhaps you are a student of history, or simply fascinated in any subject offbeat and obscure. No matter your starting point, your understanding of cemeteries will evolve with the chapters herein, even if the perspective of society at large does not progress quite as quickly.

During the years I spent directing the programming and development efforts of Laurel Hill Cemetery, a National Historic Landmark located in Philadelphia, I received one question time and again from visitors. "How on earth did you end up working in a cemetery?" was second only to the hushed and hopeful query of "Is this place haunted?" It always seemed to me that people were astonished to discover that those of us associated with cemeteries are as normal and well balanced as the average citizen. I never found the need to explain why Igor himself had not instead emerged from the cemetery office to greet visitors, dragging his limp leg at one side and a rusty shovel at the other. Those persistent assumptions about all things cemetery related were targets ripe for elimination in my work at Laurel Hill from the beginning.

Society holds death at a distance, as something foreign, instead of the constant that inevitably unites us all. Our treatment of death defines our culture as much as, if not more so, than our approach toward life. At the same time, we are currently living through an era of unparalleled societal change. Questions of identity and ideals of normalcy are being challenged daily within and across races, genders, and classes. Perhaps this age of differences and dichotomies is the perfect time to reassess our relationship with death and dying. Those questions of identity do not dissipate once life is extinguished, after all. Our legacies linger. How do you want to be remembered after you die?

To envision where the American cemetery is going, you must first appreciate where it has been. Not unlike its European precursors, the institution of the American cemetery provided the dead their right to a peaceful and perpetual rest in a setting intended for the living to enjoy. Cemeteries were once sanctuaries where families could commune with their departed loved ones amid art and nature. They preceded public parks in America, and also predated the nation's major museums, but they served the same functions in the decades between. Ultimately, cemeteries were founded for a multitude of uses, the housing of the dead being just one among them. As you'll learn throughout this text, cemeteries were originally established and embraced as sites of education, recreation, and reflection.

Fast forward to the twenty-first century. Today, the American cemetery is confronted with unprecedented challenges. Aging sites of sepulcher face issues of expansion and availability, with diminished land inadequate to sustain profitable sales. As more Americans choose cremation and accept alternative forms of committal over traditional interment, contemporary cemeteries yielding abundant space are likewise confronting an uncertain tomorrow. Cemeteries must increasingly identify new ways to ensure their relevance for current and future generations. So through innovative public programs, enhanced recreational resources, and dynamic community partnerships, the American cemetery is now returning to its roots as a destination for the living. What is past is prologue, after all.

While programming a cemetery can, of course, aid in resolving the dilemmas of diminished usage and demand, it can likewise render a new set of trials and tribulations. At this point, the vast majority of Americans has never before considered visiting a cemetery for any other purpose than to pay their respects at the grave of a friend or loved one. This contemporary national attitude was actually precipitated by events of the mid-nineteenth century, particularly the American Civil War. During the prolonged conflict, death seemed to have touched everyone to greater or lesser extents, regardless of geography or social position. By war's end, the citizenry was eager to distance itself from dying and loss. Cemeteries gradually became somber places where families could mourn lives passed as they sought to rebuild and rejuvenate their own elsewhere. The versatile uses of cemeteries became prey to time, and most present-day Americans have experienced them negatively as sites exclusive to grieving.

So we arrive upon that which makes programming a cemetery particularly arduous, as well as that which makes this book especially invaluable. In its programmatic strategy, the American cemetery may serve as museum, historic site, cultural institution, and arboretum all at once. Yet for our institutional counterparts, programming is publicly accepted and even expected. Build it, and they will come—with some proper marketing and outreach. On the other hand, to program a space that is seen as both somber and sacred, one must simultaneously convince the doubting masses of a pious purpose in doing so.

At its core, cemetery programming challenges the meaning of sacred expression. Cemetery programming is an act of remembrance and respect. It lends immortality to the lives of those whom it explores. Cemetery programming preserves the past while promising a future for so many sites of memory. It is crucial not only to convey these facts in the programming of a cemetery but also to accept and understand them yourself should you ever hope to sway those doubting masses.

Our mission in this endeavor is thus twofold. To entice audiences and patrons to take part in the entertainment that cemetery programming provides, we must also open the public's minds to cemeteries as sites of entertainment. Progress is not always linear. Oftentimes, to move forward at all, we can place the cart nowhere but before that proverbial horse and then wait in hope for the creature to take a cue and walk around. Our endeavor is twice as difficult but, alas, is often the most rewarding. Anything worthwhile never does come easy. And if you can make a cemetery one of the liveliest places in your town, you can likely do just about anything. In summation, do keep reading, as this text composes an opportunity to effect a new cultural understanding of cemeteries. It references and examines many of the most impactful programmatic methods currently being used by cemeteries across the nation, exploring their vast educational, recreational, and reflective public uses. In doing so, this text remains faithful to the history of the American cemetery, while celebrating the potential of its future as a place of profound meaning and purpose for the living.

Looking back on my first days and weeks at a then-quiet and unfrequented Laurel Hill, I saw potential unlimited but unrealized. Here was the intersection of thousands upon thousands of personal, local, and national narratives just waiting to be told. Here was the amalgamation of acres upon acres of art, architecture, and horticulture just waiting to be seen. And at the other side of the gate stood a largely unaware public, just waiting to be engaged, educated, and entertained. The interpretive lens is relative, and its reach therefore unlimited. History is not static, and our changing present will continue to reinform the past as much as the past informs today and tomorrow. In cemetery programming, I saw that the possibilities were endless. They remain so.

As I reflect in writing this foreword, I can't help but draw the comparison in that, as much as I embraced cemeteries for the opportunities they presented, Rachel Wolgemuth embraced them in outward appreciation, fascination, even affection. Though we entered the company around the same time, Rachel was studying cemeteries long before she obtained her position with Laurel Hill's sister site, West Laurel Hill in Montgomery County, Pennsylvania. In our respective positions, we grappled firsthand with the unique and often disparate issues confronting both historic and contemporary cemeteries at two of the nation's premier resting places. Over the many years we worked together, her deep knowledge of cemeteries was always apparent, always admired. During our many conversations and collaborations, it was clear to me that what was a career or job for most of us was so much more for my colleague.

I'd describe the work of cemeteries as Rachel life's work. I'd describe this book as a reflection of her devotion, intellect, and wisdom, and as a testament to her passion for and knowledge of the subject at hand. I've met my fair share of cemetery enthusiasts, but few as deeply invested in where cemeteries have been and, just as importantly, where they are going. I will remain always grateful to Rachel for the opportunity to be part of this important text, and honored to stand with her, side by side at this juncture in the ever unfolding history of the American cemetery.

Reader, as you begin this journey, remember that you can't please everybody all of the time. Not everyone will agree with the programming of cemeteries, so focus on engaging and retaining those who understand its need and value. Then, build support for this vital movement with the help of their open minds and words of mouth. Be assured that if you're not displeasing someone, you're probably not doing anything of note. And if you're not taking risks and testing boundaries, you're probably not going anywhere worth mentioning.

As you begin this journey, remember that the American cemetery's greatest challenge is also its greatest asset. As chiseled and landscaped repositories of the dead, cemeteries carry the content of endless life narratives, the weight of eras and ethos. Yes, they are museum, historic site, cultural institution, and arboretum all at once. They are garden, public park, gallery, classroom, playground, and archive to boot. One idea bears inexhaustible story lines that can be interpreted and reinterpreted a million and one ways. Be excited. Every cemetery bears boundless programmatic possibilities.

Finally, as you begin this journey, remember that what is past is prologue. History does repeat itself, and the American cemetery can be what it once was. A cultural shift is already taking place, slowly but surely, as a result of the efforts of those sites that—be it by choice or necessity—have begun to meet the challenges of the twenty-first-century American cemetery. This text may well help to hasten and expand those efforts. One need not merely live through history, after all. We are the minds and hands and voices that make it happen. The history of the American cemetery is coming full circle. We stand poised now, on the cusp of a renaissance.

Gwen Kaminski
former director of development and programming, 2005–2014
Laurel Hill Cemetery, Philadelphia, Pennsylvania

Preface

Cemeteries are cultural texts. They can show us evidence of the beliefs and values of the communities they serve just as they illuminate more mundane elements of existence such as work and family structure. While once cemeteries were multifaceted spaces used for meditation, education, and even recreation, gradual commercialization and professionalism transformed burial grounds into spaces one-dimensional in purpose. The twenty-first century has witnessed many become places of neglect due to the rise in cremation coupled with increased maintenance costs and, sometimes, mismanagement of funds. With this, we lose a place to reconnect and remember the dead. We lose a place for quiet contemplation. We lose access to one of the tools to better help us understand our past.

Faced with funds unequal to tackle mounting maintenance costs, some cemeteries are turning to tours and programming with the intention of creating a base of support for the cemetery. They hope that by using their local cemetery for tours and programs, the community will become reinvested in the space and recognize the importance of saving it, through volunteer hours, membership, or monetary contributions. Cemetery programming becomes a form of cemetery preservation. This text is intended to be a tool for cemetery staff, educators, members of historical organizations, and members of the general public looking to use their local cemetery for alternative uses. While the concept of using a cemetery for multiple purposes is not original, it is only within the past ten to fifteen years that it has once again become more common across the United States. There are countless books detailing cemetery history, art, and gravestone symbolism, but none reimagine what burial grounds can be through the creation of innovative tours and programming.

Cemetery Tours and Programming: A Guide examines the various opportunities for alternative uses of cemeteries in the form of education, recreation, and reflection. Chapter 1 provides background and historical context for the programming possibilities of today. The early nineteenth-century rural cemeteries were developed not just as places for the disposal of the dead, but also to be places for meditation and reflection, schools for learning, parks for recreation, and art museums and gardens. To understand the possibilities for today's cemetery programming, we only need to look to these predecessors of the modern cemetery. Chapter 2 examines opportunities for education in a cemetery by detailing how to create and develop walking tours. This chapter looks at each step of the process, from research to tour development to execution. The chapter concludes with two case studies of cemeteries using their spaces to educate groups of children. Chapter 3, the cemetery as a park space, examines the various opportunities for recreational activities. Chapter 4 discusses ceremonial programming and how cemeteries can develop and enhance these kinds of programs, and it closes with a case study of a Dia de los Muertos event. Chapter 5 addresses ways to market cemetery programs to the public.

This book was developed from visits to cemeteries across the country and interviews with cemetery programming coordinators. It builds on a decade of experience in creating, implementing, and leading cemetery tours and programs. The tours and programs currently occurring throughout the country are diverse, ranging from a general history walking tour to a fire arts demonstration. The institutions creating these programs are also diverse. Some conduct few new burials and consequently rely on programming, membership, and grants to remain solvent. Others use programming to help market the cemetery to prospective customers and to remain relevant to their communities. The staff, volunteers, and educators visiting cemeteries for tours or creating events for the public share the belief in the value of these sites, whether for honoring our ancestors, understanding our past, or better understanding our society. It is my hope that readers will share these beliefs, and come to understand cemeteries (and their possibilities) in a new way.

Acknowledgments

All over the country, there are smart and dedicated women and men working to preserve their local burial grounds and share the stories of those buried there. Many are working with little to no staff and a small or nonexistent budget. Many more are volunteers, teachers, and community leaders who see an underused but vital cultural resource. Throughout this project, I have been inspired by many of these people who shared their time, experience, and vision with me.

I am deeply indebted to Gwen Kaminski. Her work in nine years at Laurel Hill Cemetery influences not just me, but countless others across the country. Not only am I regularly inspired by the work Gwen has done, she contributed immensely and selflessly to this project with her feedback, suggestions, edits, and support.

The staff and volunteers (both past and present) of Laurel Hill and the Friends of Laurel Hill Cemetery were immensely supportive, both in sharing their knowledge and experiences but also in terms of helping me locate archival materials, photographs, and in providing manuscript feedback. Thank you to Alexis Jeffcoat, Michael Brooks, Dave Horwitz, Russ Dodge, and Terri Greenberg for sharing experience gleaned over years (and in some cases decades) of leading tours at Laurel Hill. Special thanks to Carol Yaster for manuscript feedback, helping me locate archival materials, and overall support and enthusiasm for this project. Thank you to Frank Rausch for sharing your beautiful photography with me. I am particularly indebted to Emma Stern, who was a consistent supporter of this project (and of me) along every step of the way, from brainstorming to photograph selection.

I feel very fortunate to have spent a decade working at a premier cemetery, and have learned a great deal from a number of smart and progressive colleagues at West Laurel Hill Cemetery. Thank you to Pete Hoskins for supporting this project, and to my colleagues from whom I have learned so much.

Thank you to Wilson and Barbara Smith for providing me with background information on the early years of the Friends of Laurel Hill and the Gravediggers' Ball.

A number of cemetery programmers have generously supported this project by spending time answering numerous questions about nearly every aspect of programming. I am regularly inspired by their vision, commitment, and generosity. I owe special thanks to Robin Simonton of Historic Oakwood Cemetery, Kim McCollum of Elmwood Cemetery, Mary Woodlan of Historic Oakland Cemetery, and Chelsea Dowell of Green-Wood Cemetery. My questions were seemingly endless, and I am deeply grateful for their assistance.

I called upon many cemeteries for this project. Thank you to Suzanne Doonan and the staff of Riverside Cemetery in Macon, Georgia; David Gilliam and Kelly Wilbanks of Hollywood Cemetery; Bree Harvey of Mount Auburn Cemetery; Beverly Lucas of Cedar Hill Cemetery; Lauren Maloy of Congressional Cemetery; Pamela Henman of Historic Oakland Cemetery; and Stacy Locke of Green-Wood Cemetery.

Thank you to Gregg Gorton for providing insights on birding in cemeteries and for your enthusiastic support for this book.

Thank you to Mark LaRocca-Pitts of Death Café Atlanta for sharing your experiences with bringing a death café to a cemetery.

Thank you Marleen Duley and Heather Wolfe for listening to my progress reports and helping with stumbling blocks.

Thank you to Jessica Dorman. I am fortunate to have such a kind, generous, and brilliant friend willing to spend countless hours in support of this project. Thank you.

Finally, I thank my parents and sisters, all of whom have acted as research assistants on various cemetery expeditions throughout the years.

Introduction
Before You Begin

Across the country, historians, teachers, educators, and community organizers are increasingly using cemeteries as stages for diverse activities. They may be inspired by the beautiful art and architecture, quiet and unused space, sense of history, or the unconscious need many humans have to confront death and their own mortality. In many instances, the motivation to develop tours or programs comes from a place of necessity, as cemeteries fill and revenue no longer is sufficient to maintain the spaces. Regardless of motivation, the beginning of the twenty-first century has witnessed a return of the cemetery as a multidimensional space to be used beyond merely burial. This increase in cemetery walking tours, programs, and events demonstrates the public's willingness to experience and understand the cemetery in a new way.

Creating cemetery programming poses a unique set of challenges, as cemeteries are environments unlike any other. They are spaces embedded within our communities yet set apart from daily life. They provide a practical service to society by acting as spaces for the disposal of the dead, yet are held, by many, to be among the most sacred spaces on earth. They are both oriented to the past and designed to speak to future generations. To create effective programming, it is useful to understand the types of cemeteries found across America; some of the unique challenges faced by those wanting to expand how a cemetery is used; and some of the resources and information available to build a foundation for creating tours and programming in cemeteries.

Cemetery Types

One of the challenges in creating cemetery programming is the diversity in types of cemeteries, types of ownership, condition of the burial grounds, and amount of documentation and related materials available to researchers. With more than 150,000 separate burial grounds in the United States composing around two million acres,[1] there are ample opportunities for cemetery programming. Nearly every community has a burial ground. But while every burial ground is a potential teaching tool or space for programming, not every cemetery is accessible and available for use by the public. The types of cemeteries in a community will vary depending upon several factors, including the size of the community, age, ethnic and religious composition of the population, and wealth of the community. Below is a partial list of some of the main types of formally organized burial grounds and cemeteries across the nation.

- *Family Graveyards.* Particularly in rural areas, small family graveyards were constructed on private land. These burial grounds frequently become victims of suburban sprawl and risk being moved to make way for commercial or residential development.
- *Churchyards.* In many parts of America, the most popular form of burial up until the establishment of the rural cemetery was the churchyard. These burial grounds, maintained by the church or religious governing organization, are usually found adjacent to a church building.
- *Rural Cemeteries.* Established beginning in the 1830s, these cemeteries revolutionized the way Americans buried their dead, even bringing the word *cemetery* into the American lexicon. Acting as the first municipal parks, many of these sites have retained their lush plantings and beautiful statuary. Even though the look of the rural cemetery would begin to fall out of favor after the 1860s, their popularity would permanently alter the way Americans buried their dead.
- *Lawn Park Cemeteries.* A response to the complaint that the rural cemeteries were too cluttered and crowded, the "landscape lawn plan," developed beginning in 1855 by Adolph Strauch of Spring Grove Cemetery in Cincinnati, Ohio, featured open, grassy lawn spaces. This style was adopted throughout the United States, often in cemeteries that functioned as commercial, for-profit ventures.
- *Municipal Cemeteries.* Owned by a local government, these are frequently nondenominational in nature.
- *Religious/Ethnic Cemeteries.* These cemeteries were founded based on a unifying ethnic and/or religious background. While many are still maintained by that founding body, in some instances (for example,

the Philadelphia Catholic Cemeteries), their management has been sold or leased to a corporate for-profit organization.
- *Veterans' Cemeteries.* Both state and national veterans' cemeteries maintain eligibility requirements for veterans and their families.
- *Fraternal Organizations' Cemeteries.* Membership-based organizations such as the Masons or Odd Fellows have established cemeteries for members and their families.

For the purposes of this book, a rural cemetery was used as the model for the kinds of tours and programming cemeteries can host. As this book was written from the point of view of a larger cemetery, not all activities will translate to all burial grounds, but the hope is that the types of events and programs mentioned in this guide can serve as inspiration. This book was also written primarily from the point of view of those who work in/for cemeteries, but it is also intended for those who could work with them— virtually anyone in the community. You could join a friends group, you could partner your company or your nonprofit with a cemetery, or you could be a teacher looking to engage students. Not all activities will translate to every circumstance, but hopefully they will inspire anyone seeking to use their local cemetery in a new way.

Before You Begin

In many states, cemetery governance is (and has been) minimal, perhaps a contributing factor to the neglect found in so many cemeteries. Before creating any type of cemetery tour, it is essential to determine the ownership of the cemetery and to gain permission to conduct a tour. Cemeteries can be privately owned, owned by the city or local government, owned by a church or archdiocese, or corporately owned by an entity located thousands of miles away. If you are interested in giving a tour inside a cemetery where there is already a robust tour program, expect script approval or authorization to be a condition upon which permission is granted.

It is also useful to be aware that cemeteries (and the deceased) were once moved with a great deal of frequency. While this may still occur today, particularly in formerly rural areas where a great deal of development is occurring, it is rare to see an entire burial ground moved to a new location all at one time. When you are conducting research for the cemetery you are using, you might also need to research long-defunct burial grounds to understand the origins of the deceased.

In Defense of Cemetery Programming

Members of a community are bound to have vastly different opinions when confronted with the idea of using a cemetery for something other than burial because Americans have widely disparate feelings about the spaces. Some believe entering a cemetery will bring bad luck, others are frightened of ghosts and the spirits of ancestors, and still others find the very notion of even walking across the grave of a deceased person to be disrespectful. Active cemeteries may be emotionally laden places for those who have recently lost a loved one. For the religious, they may be thought to be spiritual places used to commune with the dead by bringing gifts or through prayer and meditation. For others, they act as outdoor museums or cultural artifacts. And while in the minority, some individuals attach no particular spiritual meaning or significance to these locations and instead simply view them as repositories for bones and stones, or a waste of valuable real estate. No matter where the programming creators and those conducting programs lie on the spirituality spectrum, it is essential to realize *most* humans view cemeteries as sacred spaces where the dead should be shown a measure of respect. What "respect" exactly means is up to interpretation and debate, and deciphering this can depend upon knowing your community and audience.

In her comprehensive book *The American Resting Place*, Marilyn Yalom expresses concern that there are "reasons to fear" some programming activities will "desacralize" the cemetery and "make it a form of fun park" to meet "commercial ends."[2] What Yalom fails to mention is that the vast majority of nonprofit cemeteries, cemetery foundations, and cemetery friends groups are conducting programming as a matter of survival. Some have endowments barely large enough to sustain the level of maintenance required just to cut the grass and maintain safe spaces.

Yalom's fears, however, are common among many Americans when they are first confronted with the idea of nontraditional activities occurring in a cemetery. They fear what Yalom describes, but there is a more fundamental concern below the surface. If our cemeteries are no longer considered "sacred" spaces, what does it mean for the value of our own lives? Most Americans will be forgotten within a few generations of their deaths (within one hundred years). Contemplating mortality and the loss of the "sacred" cemetery space to remember ancestors can be a frightening thought for those concerned with being remembered after their deaths.

Rather than "desacralizing" cemetery space, however, programs do the exact opposite. By bringing people into the space, we are forced to remember and acknowledge our ancestors. A walking tour could illuminate a life forgotten for decades or centuries. Cemetery programming can be the best form of historic preservation. Having visitors regularly use the cemetery not only helps to instill a love and appreciation for the burial ground but also provides security. Regular visitors are often the ones to alert staff to potential nefarious activities, storm damage, or other maintenance issues. Events can help garner volunteers for gardening, research, or other work in support of the cemetery. Revenue generated from events in the form of donations or tour fees can help pay for maintaining the spaces. Cemeteries such as Laurel Hill, in Philadelphia, have used cemetery programming to generate revenue, increase membership, and, more importantly, regenerate the community's respect for the space. In the past fifteen years, the cemetery has worked to grow and expand the number and diversity of tours and programs. During that time, membership in the Friends of Laurel Hill has increased nearly fourfold. Membership is an indicator not just of revenue generated but also of the level of interest and participation in the cemetery's activities. Laurel Hill is once again a culturally relevant, vital part of the Philadelphia landscape. Without the activities conducted by the Friends of Laurel Hill, and the support of the staff and management of the Cemetery Company in supporting creative programming, the cemetery would have a hard time sustaining itself into the twenty-first century. We change and evolve. We need to reevaluate and shift our perceptions of what it means to honor and respect something perceived as "sacred," and recognize that there are varied ways to respect cemetery space and the deceased buried within.

At the same time, without careful supervision and planning, tours can, at times, put a cemetery at risk. Unsupervised children might try to climb on monuments. If a cemetery doesn't have at least basic security (a locking gate), drawing attention to stained glass windows, bronze doors, and other artwork can potentially alert thieves. This balance is something to be considered when bringing tours and programming to a cemetery. In 2015 the archdiocese of New Orleans closed the cemetery St. Louis No. 1 to visitors unless they are accompanied by a licensed tour guide due to the continued vandalism at the tomb of Marie Laveau, the "voodoo queen" of New Orleans. The constant visitation and legend surrounding a wish-granting ritual done at the tomb has led to vandalism and destruction. While New Orleans cemeteries are tourist attractions and visits to these cemeteries generate both interest and revenue, the risk to the cemeteries became too great. Before you undertake any cemetery tours or programming, be aware of potential security issues and do your best to address those concerns prior to inviting increasing numbers of people into the cemetery.

Surveys and Recommended Reading

In order to create a cemetery tour or program, you should start by determining if the cemetery has been surveyed, if a map and or plan of the property exists, and what records exist. If the burial ground has been dormant for a long period of time and no records can be found, consult your state or local agencies for laws and regulations for documenting and surveying the site. Appendix A is a listing of state historic preservation offices and organizations focused on cemetery preservation and documentation. While there is a great deal of variance on the types of resources available online, many of these websites offer guides and forms for recording and surveying a cemetery. When creating historic cemetery tours, it helps to have a general knowledge of trends in American cemetery history, gravestone types, and symbolism along with local or regional trends in memorialization. A solid foundation in local or regional history will help you develop tours the local community can connect to. Consult Appendix B for some recommended reading and suggested reference guides. Many of the state websites noted in Appendix A also provide information on local types of cemeteries, markers, and symbolism found within the state. In addition,

Introduction 1.   Laurel Hill Cemetery overlooking the Schuylkill River.
Photo by Emma Stern.

the Association for Gravestone Studies (http://www.gravestonestudies
.org) provides access to a great quantity of regional information and studies,
in part through free online access to *Markers*, its journal.

Cemeteries are important spaces. They help us deal with loss and come
to terms with death. They are places where we can perform the ceremonies and rituals that tie us to our ethnic, religious, or cultural roots. They
are records of our past. We program cemeteries to preserve them, and we
preserve them, in part, to learn from them. Noted folklorist and cemetery
scholar Richard E. Meyer perhaps has explained it best. We study cemeteries and gravemarkers "for the same reasons, in essence, that we value and
study all artifacts which embody lasting cultural truths: to help us achieve a
better understanding of ourselves—what we are, what we have been, and,
perhaps, what we are in the process of becoming."[3]

Notes

1. Eggener, *Cemeteries*, 37.
2. Yalom, *The American Resting Place*, 276.
3. Meyer, *Cemeteries & Gravemarkers*, 5.

Background and History   1

Americans tend to think of cemeteries as static and unchanging. We use the phrase *etched in stone* to imply permanence. In fact, not only do cemeteries change over time in terms of layout, composition, and structure, they also reflect changes in communities and our larger society. Their physical appearance may change as the ethnic and religious composition or prosperity of a region shifts. Broader cultural influences or movements in art and architecture influence cemetery buildings and monuments. In addition to reflecting change, a cemetery's very purpose may expand or contract over time as shifts in our culture occur. What we think of as a typical cemetery is only a glimpse into the ever-evolving way we bury the dead. The cemetery is a reflection of the living population it serves, and as such, it will change to reflect the needs of those it serves.

Since the beginning of the twentieth century, cemeteries have been largely used for one purpose: burial of the dead. Conducting tours and programming in these spaces might strike some as odd or even disrespectful to the dead. Often the only exposure Americans have had to a cemetery—to attend a family member's burial service, to place flowers on a friend's grave—conjures strong and perhaps unsettling emotions. And yet the American cemetery was once an important cultural institution, serving needs beyond body disposal. The tours and programming some cemeteries across the nation are beginning to develop have roots in the new form of burial established in the 1830s in the "rural cemetery." Apart from being places for the interment of the dead, these cemeteries were intended to be places for reflection, recreation, and education. To understand the types of tours and programming we can develop in today's cemeteries, it helps to first look at their historical roots.

In the early nineteenth century, the word *cemetery* (Greek for "sleeping place") was not a regular part of the American vocabulary. Burial grounds in urban areas were overcrowded, dismal places, to be avoided. In cities like Boston, Baltimore, New York, and Philadelphia, burial grounds were frequently moved to make room for the expansion of homes and businesses. Boston graveyards were so overcrowded, burials were occurring four-deep or in small, common trenches. Since not every grave was marked, new interments often disturbed previous ones. Grave robbing (stealing corpses for the medical "profession") and vandalism were frequent occurrences.[1]

Movements started by civic-minded, educated, well-connected individuals in cities such as Boston led to the establishment of the rural cemetery, a revolutionary new model for burial (beginning with Mount Auburn in Cambridge, Massachusetts, in 1831, and Laurel Hill Cemetery in Philadelphia, in 1836). These new spaces, located several miles outside the city, soon became immensely popular, and the word *cemetery* was more commonly used. To be certain, a primary consideration for the establishment of America's first cemeteries was utility. These rural cemeteries would accommodate the burial needs of a growing population by providing ample space for future burials, well beyond the confines of the growing city. Advocates also sought to address health concerns, as it was thought that by removing the dead from the space of the living, sanitation would improve and disease and epidemics caused by "bad air" would decline.

But just as cemeteries were developed to serve the very real physical needs of an expanding population, the founders also knew cemeteries would be an integral part of a community's fabric, serving not just as burial grounds for the dead but also as refuges for the living population. They would be places to stroll amid nature and reflect on the meanings of life and death. In a time when few cities had public parks and museums, cemeteries would be places providing cultural enrichment. These new cemeteries were intended to be places of instruction where the joint combination of fine art and horticulture would educate and inspire all visitors, not just artists and writers. When visiting these "didactic landscapes," visitors "absorbed lessons on nature and its cycles, on mortality, humility, morality, and charity."[2] In a time when the last of the Revolutionary War veterans were dying, rural cemetery founders looked for ways to stake claim to a heritage that would inspire patriotism in future generations. They believed that monuments noting the accomplishments of the famous would exude a positive influence on Americans strolling the paths and contemplating the lives and work of those buried beneath them.

These beliefs can be found in the rhetoric used to support this radical new style of burial. In an address published in the Boston papers, politician and orator Edward Everett advocated for the establishment of a new kind of burial ground where visitors could come to "contemplate without dread or disgust" in safety, "secure from the danger of being encroached upon" and "removed from all the discordant scenes of life."[3] Similarly, in an address given at the dedication of Mount Auburn Cemetery on September 24, 1831, Supreme Court Justice Joseph Story laid out several of the purposes for the space beyond disposal of the dead. "Our Cemeteries rightly selected, and properly arranged, may be made subservient to some of the highest purposes of religion and human duty. They may preach lessons, to which none may refuse to listen, and which all, that live, must hear."[4] He sees many of these lessons being revealed by contrasting the city of the living (Boston) with the city of the dead (the cemetery), and notes Boston, in the distance across the Charles River, as "at once the object of our admiration and our love" as it "rears its proud eminences, its glittering spires, its lofty towers, its graceful mansions, its curling smoke, its crowded haunts of business and pleasure, which speak to the eye, and yet leave a noiseless loneliness on the ear."[5] He is both speaking with fondness of the many attractions of the city and letting the audience know these pleasures come at a price.

The crowds who visited Mount Auburn and the other rural cemeteries in those first years, however, often came as much for recreation as for reverence. In her account of the founding of Mount Auburn, Blanche Linden notes that as America's "first designed fantasy landscape," Mount Auburn appealed to those seeking a sense of "mystical excitement and even adventure," and visitors found both by wandering the winding paths of the varied terrain of the cemetery.[6] Soon established in communities across the nation, these early rural cemeteries became tourist attractions and "must-see" destinations for visitors. On weekends, city dwellers escaped to cemeteries to stroll along the winding paths, lounge in the grass, or picnic. Cemeteries like Mount Auburn and Laurel Hill even issued guidebooks.

An estimated 140,000 people visited Laurel Hill Cemetery in 1860, and the administration began issuing tickets and restricting admission.[7] Brooklyn's Green-Wood Cemetery was attracting one hundred thousand visitors per year in the 1850s, and by the 1860s that number was up to five hundred thousand.[8] In fact, so many "tourists" were patronizing these new cemeteries that management often put rules in place regarding the speed of carriages and prohibiting picnicking, firearms, and "talking

GUIDE
TO
LAUREL HILL CEMETERY

PHILADELPHIA

1844.

J. Notman, Arch.t & del.t   EAST WINDOW of CHAPEL.

Lith. of Pinkerton Wagner & Mc Guigan Philadelphia

Figure 1.1.   Guide to Laurel Hill Cemetery, 1844.
Source: Laurel Hill Cemetery.

loudly" on Sundays.[9] Visitors to Mount Auburn gathered flowers and mutilated trees (for whittling), prompting the cemetery to post signs and eventually fine violators.[10] Unfortunately, these rules were often difficult to enforce. The tension between funerals and recreation would be felt by most of the first-generation rural cemeteries.

By the end of the nineteenth century, however, changes had occurred to more narrowly define the role of the American cemetery. The staggering loss of life generated by the Civil War obliterated the sentimentalism surrounding death. Municipal parks—their development spurred in part by the popularity of the rural cemetery movement—gradually claimed cemeteries' recreational patronage. Museums and galleries became the repositories of American art and sculpture, and botanical gardens and arboreta the horticultural showpieces.

The "process of death" was gradually removed from the hands of the family and placed into the hands of "professionals." The rural cemeteries had initiated these changes by having a paid staff, rules and restrictions, and enclosing the cemetery space, but this trend continued as cemeteries put more limits on an individual's involvement in a burial and in memorialization. To further improve the management and control over the cemeteries they supervised, the Association of American Cemetery Superintendents was created in 1887. This coincided with the increase in the number of for-profit cemeteries, and as the number of cemeteries created between the 1870s and 1920s dramatically increased, many of these new ventures were commercial endeavors.[11]

Figure 1.2.   Men lounging in Green-Wood Cemetery.
Source: Green-Wood Historic Fund Collection.

The rise in the funeral industry following the Civil War further removed death, as the first funeral homes began to appear and Americans turned to undertakers for burial of the dead. Undertakers became more popular as embalming became used more frequently, and gradually, over time, funerals were no longer held in the home. In addition, by the 1880s, a greater percentage of Americans died in hospitals than at home.[12] Where once, loved ones had cared for family members at home until they died and been deeply involved with every aspect of the rituals following death, commercial entities were emerging to strip them of those responsibilities.

As some historians have argued, Americans were also becoming more "forgetful and detached"[13] not only from death but also from elements of their own history. In his classic 1991 survey of the history of American cemeteries, David Charles Sloane notes that while once burial grounds were moved with little consideration, all in the name of progress and urban expansion, today it is next to impossible to uproot an existing burial ground. But ironically, "as the grave has become legally inviolate, Americans have become increasingly indifferent to the cemetery as a sacred space or as a community and cultural institution. The cemetery's role as a repository of the history and memories of the local community is fading."[14] The stories illustrated by the art, architecture, and horticulture are now told by museums, art galleries, and botanical gardens. The roles in fostering community and identity have been rescinded, the cemetery's functional diversity replaced with the utilitarian role of disposal.

As the twenty-first century begins, cemeteries are facing increasing pressures regarding their relevance and sustainability. More and more Americans—a percentage expected to top 50 percent by 2018[15]—are embracing cremation, and many are more interested in the practical disposal of the dead than in the ceremonial aspects of burial and memorialization. Memorial Day, once a time for visiting a cemetery to pay tribute to the dead, is now more frequently thought of as a signal for the start of summer. While in the past, Americans tended to stay connected to a community for several generations, many today live far from their parents, and the attachment to a local burial ground is lost. Often, what used to be a locally run cemetery is now managed by a large corporation located in another state, its leadership accountable to shareholders rather than to the community the cemetery serves. As time goes on, a cemetery costs more and more money to maintain; open land becomes used for burials, and eventually monuments sink and become worn and roads need to be paved and maintained. Many cemeteries have fallen into disrepair, their profits from property and monument sales shrinking and their endowments not equal to the cost of maintaining vast acres of land.

Faced with these issues, some have established 501(c)(3) Friends groups and begun to create events and programming in an effort not only to bring in income but also to return the cemetery to a place of cultural relevance in a community. Cemeteries with few active burials use tours and programming to raise funds and increase membership, while "active" cemeteries (those still selling property and conducting burials) may use programming as a marketing tool to bring the public into the cemetery. In important ways, these are not new uses but a return to original, early nineteenth-century purposes.

Cemeteries communicate grand ideas about mortality and values. They link the past and the future, and both isolate and provide a place for communing with the dead. The founders of America's first rural cemeteries recognized this and viewed cemeteries as significant civic improvements with the potential to inspire and instruct visitors as well as to provide relief from the pressures of an increasingly industrialized society. When we consider the types of programming we can create in cemeteries, it first helps

Figure 1.3.   The view from historic Oakland Cemetery in Atlanta, Georgia.
Photo courtesy of Ren and Helen Davis.

to consider the roots of America's first cemeteries and their original uses for recreation, education, and reflection.

Notes

1. The establishment of the American Medical Association in 1847 would begin the process of establishing standards regarding education and licensure requirements, but in the early 1800s the field was largely unregulated, and protests over "resurrectionists" occurred in several American cities. One of the largest post-Revolutionary riots, the "Doctors' Riot," occurred in 1788 over the removal of corpses by doctors and medical students.

2. Eggener, *Cemeteries*, 25.

3. Bigelow, *A History of Mt. Auburn Cemetery*, 138–39.

4. Bigelow, *A History of Mt. Auburn Cemetery*, 156.

5. Bigelow, *A History of Mt. Auburn Cemetery*, 162.

6. Linden, *Silent City on a Hill*, 248.

7. Sloane, *The Last Great Necessity*, 82.

8. Richman, *Brooklyn's Green-Wood Cemetery*, 16.

9. Richman, *Brooklyn's Green-Wood Cemetery*, 19.

10. Linden-Ward, "Strange but Genteel Pleasure Grounds," 318.

11. Sloane, *The Last Great Necessity*, 133.

12. Sloane, *The Last Great Necessity*, 119.

13. Eggener, *Cemeteries*, 27.

14. Sloane, *The Last Great Necessity*, 7.

15. Cremation Association of North America.

Using the Cemetery for Education   **2**
Developing the Cemetery Tour

As a created space, a community's burial ground acts as a type of cultural text. It becomes an artifact, and as such it can be used to teach about the lives, beliefs, and values of the population it serves. The way most people learn about a cemetery is through the cemetery tour. The content of cemetery tours currently conducted throughout the country is diverse, ranging from local history to global events and the esoteric and obscure to the fundamental and universal. A number of factors—including the audience, the guide(s) giving the tour, and the amount of information currently available—determine the types of tours a given cemetery can create. This chapter begins with a methodology for gathering content for a walking tour by using cemetery records, archival paper records, digital records, and the material culture of the cemetery itself. The next section provides tips for assessing content and developing a successful cemetery walking tour. This is followed by a section on training tour guides, creating tours and activities for school groups and children, and creating digital and self-guided walking tours. The chapter is followed by two case studies of successfully using cemeteries to educate children.

Any cemetery walking tour is based upon research and an understanding of how those elements can be combined. Consider three main determinants when developing content for a cemetery tour:

- First, *Who is buried in the cemetery?* Think about this question both in terms of "famous" or well-known individuals (both locally and/or nationally) but also in broader terms of the population the cemetery has served. What stories do their lives tell, and how can these stories connect and become relevant to today's audience?

Figure 2.1.   A walking tour in Laurel Hill Cemetery, Philadelphia.
Source: Emma Stern.

- Second, *What are the notable architecture and design elements?* Are there any significant buildings, memorials, or monuments in the cemetery? Are there works by a sculptor, architect, or stone carver you think should be shared? Are there trends in art or funerary symbolism evident in the stones and monuments? What epitaphs and symbols convey beliefs and values shared by this community? What are the distinctive, eye-catching, or unique memorials in the cemetery?
- Third, *What is the natural landscape?* Rural cemeteries in particular were developed as arboreta, and many continue to have a significant collection of notable trees and plantings. Think about the horticulture and the specimens and natural elements you should or could include in a tour.

Research: Learning about the "Permanent Residents" in a Cemetery

Cemetery markers and headstones are physical representations and reminders of individuals who used to live in the community, and it is essential to find out more about who those people were. While cemetery tours can be diverse in content, the foundation is the people. When first creating a tour, there are a number of ways to find information about the people buried in the cemetery you're using. Start with cemetery records. Begin by determining if cemetery records exist, and what organization maintains and houses them. If the cemetery is still actively burying people, it is likely to create and maintain at least rudimentary records. If few or no burials are occurring, cemetery records (if they still exist) might have been moved to a local library, archive, or historical society. At other times, records can be found in the personal possession of a long-time cemetery caretaker. If the burial ground has no paper records and has never been surveyed, see the resources listed in Appendix B or in your state's listing in Appendix A. While there are certainly differences based on the type and age of the cemetery, ownership, and state requirements, there are some documents common to most professionally run cemeteries. Within those documents, however, there can be a great disparity in the amount and quality of information collected. Below are examples of records commonly found in cemetery archives.

- *Cemetery-Created Lists.* In some instances, cemeteries maintain lists of military veterans and officers or "notables" buried there. This can be a starting place for understanding not only who is buried within the gates but also what previous generations considered noteworthy.
- *Death Notices and Obituaries.* Death notices (short, paid announcements of deaths) and obituaries (longer biographies usually written by the newspaper itself rather than paid for by the family of the deceased) are sometimes clipped by cemetery staff and saved in the burial records. These are important documents, not just for confirming dates of birth and death, family, and other genealogical information, but also for providing information on the deceased's occupation, hobbies, or interests.
- *Burial Permits.* These documents, created by the cemetery, note the date of burial along with the location (section, plot, or and/or grave number) of the burial. Other information could include the charges associated with burying the deceased, the names of family or next of kin, the place of death, cause of death, and relation to the original lot owner.
- *Transit Permits.* Depending upon the year of the deceased's death, as well as where they died, the city or locality might have issued a transit permit. This permit grants permission for an undertaker (funeral director) to transport the deceased for burial in the cemetery. This

document can be useful for providing information on the dates of death or burial and also the name of the undertaker.

- *Authorization by Family.* In addition to burial permits, more recent cemetery records usually contain authorization for the burial to take place signed by the next of kin. This information creates a fuller picture of the family and can also lead to current next-of-kin contact information.
- *Lot Sketch/Plot Diagram.* Active cemeteries maintain sketches of the burials in each plot in order to see where future burials can occur. This is one of the most important documents in the cemetery vault, and as such it can be relied upon for family names and, sometimes, dates. These records can also be used to document the location of the burial of a deceased individual when no stone is present.
- *Interment Cards/Death Registers.* Cemeteries frequently maintain a type of card catalogue of deceased individuals and or/registers or logs of burials. Often, these lists contain few details other than the name, location, and date of burial. They can be useful, however, in helping to determine at what time period the cemetery was the most active (performing the most burials).
- *Deeds.* Many cemeteries issue deeds to property owners. Not only are these visually interesting documents, they sometimes provide information on the size of the property and the amount for which it was originally purchased.
- *Correspondence.* Correspondence stored in cemetery records can provide a wealth of information. The contents of the letters themselves might merely pertain to conditions of the property or an upcoming burial, but sometimes the letterhead on which they were written gives clues to the profession of the deceased or where they lived. Correspondence can confirm genealogical details, which can help create a fuller picture of the deceased. Correspondence can also provide details on the memorialization on the property (such as who constructed the monument).
- *Photographs.* Some cemeteries retain photographs of individual stones, the cemetery as a whole, and events that have occurred over the years. Cemeteries change in appearance over time. Stones fall over, bronze memorials can be stolen or removed, sculptures wear and fade, and sometimes vandalism occurs. The cemetery expands over time, and trees and vegetation grow and change. As cemetery preservation expert Lynette Strangstad notes in her text *A Graveyard Preservation Primer*, "The various features, structures, materials, and plantings found at the site, together with spatial relationships of built

features and relationships between the built features and the landscape features, all help to understand the site, the culture that shaped it, and its importance within the immediate locality and the region."[1] Photographs are one way to help recreate a picture of the original appearance of the cemetery or graveyard.

- *Maps.* Similarly, maps can help to create an awareness of the cemetery layout and how the cemetery has developed over time. Comparing older historic maps to newer ones may show buildings that were removed or added. In addition, cemetery maps may note family lot owners at key intersections or junctions in the cemetery. These names serve both as landmarks and as indicators of status. Just as in real estate for the living, cemetery properties can be more or less desirable based upon many factors, one being their location along a road or path.
- *Financial Ledgers/Receipts.* For cemeteries retaining financial ledgers, the amount paid for a cemetery plot or headstone can help indicate an individual's wealth within the context of the cemetery community.
- *Cemetery Trust/Endowment Records.* These records detail special work paid for. For example, a private mausoleum might have an endowment not just for general maintenance but also for sweeping the mausoleum weekly and providing flowers at holidays.
- *Cemetery Rules and Regulations, Price Lists, and Guide Books.* Professionally run cemeteries frequently create publications to attract new customers as well as lay out the rules of the cemetery.

Other Records

Other records that can be helpful in your search include:

- *Vital Records (Birth and Death).* Cemeteries do not typically retain a copy of the death certificate, and the institution of a formal death accounting system varies state by state. While access to these records may be limited, the search is worth the effort. In the case of Philadelphia, for example, the city established its Board of Health and first started recording deaths and burials in 1803, and continued until the state took over that responsibility in 1915. These documents of burials (or "cemetery returns") can now be accessed for free on the website http://www.familysearch.org, as can genealogical records from other locales.
- *Census Records.* Census records (available online through both free and paid sites) are useful for filling in gaps in familial relationships, as well as occupation and immigration status.
- *Military Records.*

- *City Directories*. City or local directories are helpful both in confirming a decedent and in identifying the undertakers, stonemasons, and other individuals/industries associated with the process of burial.
- *Probate Records*.
- *Burial Society Records*. In Jewish communities, burial societies were responsible for making sure members received a proper Jewish burial. The society would purchase a group of plots for its members and then administer the reselling of the graves. While many of these organizations are now defunct, efforts exist in places such as New York to document the names and locations of all burial-society-owned plots.[2] Be aware that other religious groups may also organize burial societies to ensure their members are buried together and in accordance with tradition or doctrine, and in these instances, surviving records could prove useful.

For churchyards and burial grounds once or currently affiliated with a church, the church or diocese might maintain records. Similarly, a synagogue whose members used a designated burial ground might maintain records of burials. For other cemeteries and graveyards, few paper records providing details on the lives of the deceased have survived. If the congregation the cemetery served is no longer in existence, it may prove difficult to locate records even if they still exist. In these cases, researchers must turn to other sources and repositories such as historical societies, libraries, or archives to retrieve obituary information or lists of local burials. Local libraries frequently house biographical encyclopedias. Both independent bookstores and chains usually have a "local history" or "local interest" section. Local history texts are vital references to the people and pivotal events in the community. Cross-referencing the names in these books against cemetery burial records to see how many matches you find can be tedious, but the results are frequently fruitful, creating a fuller picture of the deceased's life. Keep in mind, however, that these texts are filled with the stories of rich, white, Protestant men. Finding records on women and society's less powerful members is usually a tougher task.

A Note about Genealogy

Genealogists can be some of the most persistent and detail-oriented people around, often scouring cemeteries across the country in search of their family history. They will exhaust every avenue to confirm the identity of a long-lost ancestor. When looking for information on the deceased buried in a cemetery, genealogists and genealogy websites can certainly be vital in confirming a burial and providing documentation. At the same time,

genealogists are often more concerned with the challenge of linking ancestors across generations, and they are less concerned with understanding
the lives of those people, placing their stories in a greater historical context
and using them to learn and teach the current generation. The records and
documentation accumulated by genealogists can be incredibly helpful in
filling out a fuller picture of the deceased, but it is important to be aware
of the limitations of genealogy as a sole or primary resource.

Digital Sources

The Internet is usually a good place to continue the search for who is
buried in a cemetery. While in the past, searching newspapers for records
of deaths involved hours of paging through microfilm, digital resources
make searching much easier today. The National Endowment for the
Humanities and the Library of Congress have sponsored "Chronicling
America" to digitize and provide access to newspapers from 1836 to1922
(http://chroniclingamerica.loc.gov/). You can type in your cemetery or
burial ground's name to access obituaries and death notices. In addition,
many colleges and universities maintain digital newspaper archives. Often
libraries have searchable obituary databases you can access from the Internet. These can be used to search for a cemetery or to try to confirm that
someone is buried in that cemetery by locating his or her death notice
or obituary. If the graveyard or cemetery you are looking into does not
have a website, a useful way to find names is through the website http://
www.findagrave.com. Find a Grave allows searching by cemetery not just
to find the "famous," but it also lists names (and sometimes photos) of the
people buried within, and it allows users to post biographical information
and photos. Another website, http://www.politicalgraveyard.com, lists the
locations of burials of politicians, judges, and diplomats. Both of these sites
are helpful for cross-referencing names and also to help you discover if
someone "famous" is buried in the cemetery you are researching. Another
digital source is Google Books. Google Books at https://books.google.
com/books allows searchers to find and preview millions of books from
around the world. Many books in the public domain have also been digitized and can be downloaded at no charge. Even if no digitized version
is available for download, simply having access to the citation is a helpful
pointer to use to track down a physical copy.

Other Sources

Another way to find information on who is buried in a cemetery is to talk to
former and current caretakers, staff, and volunteers (if there is a staff of any

kind). Often the people who work day after day among the stones know best who is buried there. Caretakers may know family stories, where noteworthy individuals are buried, or the location of the most interesting monuments or epitaphs. Unfortunately, this information is often locked in their memory until someone takes the time to record these stories. From the starting point of a story, a researcher can move to other sources to fill in the gaps of a biography or to confirm facts and details. For cemeteries maintaining lists of current contacts and lot owners, a simple letter asking for biographical and genealogical information can yield great results. Family historians often welcome the chance to share their discoveries with a willing listener, and they are often the source to alert us to a long-forgotten family member with an interesting story. A similar "call for information" letter or online posting to a local historical society or a library can yield results. For cemeteries with websites, offering a place to submit biographical information can result in a deluge of submissions of family history. In addition to requesting family information, ask if descendants would be willing to share letters, diaries, or other documents to help create a more complete picture of the deceased.

Material Culture: Learning to Decipher the Stories in the Stones

> *Material culture is made up of tangible things crafted, shaped, altered, and used across time and across space. It is inherently personal and social, mental and physical.*
>
> —SIMON J. BRONNER, *AMERICAN MATERIAL CULTURE AND FOLKLIFE: A PROLOGUE AND DIALOGUE*

Americans memorialize their dead with marble, bronze, or granite markers. Sometimes, and among certain religious or ethnic communities such as the Quakers and the Amish, the gravestones are uniform in size and shape and have similar script and content. They are used simply as markers for the burial location of the dead, only displaying the most rudimentary information. This in itself, however, says as much about the deceased and her community as the most complicated memorial. The stones, inscriptions, and memorials erected by the deceased or by surviving family members communicate the beliefs, fears, and personality of the person buried beneath—but also illuminate the community she was a part of. Gravestones and their relation to one another in the graveyard or cemetery convey identity. They are frequently the last created reminder of a life, and these material artifacts "serve as tangible intermediaries in the ongoing communicative process leading to a richer understanding of the history and cultural values of community, region and nation."[3] If gravestones are part of a "system drawing together maker, user, and apprehender,"[4] they hold clues for understanding not only the deceased and the creators of the stone but also ourselves. How we understand that creation and how we explain it can be revelatory. Understanding how to use the stones themselves as primary texts is crucial in developing dynamic walking tours.

Group Data: Examining the Cemetery as a Community

In many ways, a cemetery is a type of community. It is a group whose members were united in death by having something in common during life, whether it was religion, race, ethnicity, socioeconomic class, or locality. It is essential to attempt to understand what common factors existed to bring these people together into one cemetery. At times, the answer is simple and obvious. A churchyard, for example, buried members of a particular church or religion. A particular language could identify the burial ground as an ethnicity-tied cemetery. At other times, however, the only uniting factor appears to be that the deceased lived in the same town or geographical area.

A cemetery community can also be analyzed for demographic and sociological data. In their article "The Adkins-Woodson Cemetery: A Sociological Examination of Cemeteries as Communities," Gary S. Foster and Richard L. Hummel make the argument that cemeteries can be used as tools for gathering sociological data, and whose populations can be described demographically. Gender, mortality rates, age, ethnicity, and family relationships are all data available to collectors.[5] In addition, there are times when a burial ground is all that's left of the population it served. In the absence of paper records and other artifacts, the cemetery can act as the primary source for information. While few cemetery tour planners will have the time to analyze birth and death rates, epidemics, and mortality rates, the idea of "reading" the whole cemetery and looking for and analyzing patterns in the numbers is an intriguing approach to understanding a burial ground, and it reminds us to avoid thinking solely in terms of individual stones or family plots and to consider the entire cemetery as a community.

Individual Data: Identifying the Individual's Position within the Community

Researchers can also use the cemetery to help determine an individual's place or status within that community by examining individual stones and their relationship to others in the cemetery.

- *Location or Placement of Grave.* Prior to examining an individual stone, examining the very *location* of a burial can tell you something about the deceased. Is the gravesite on a hill or prominent overlook? Is it along a path or road? Is it isolated by a path, fencing, or other type of enclosure? How does its orientation relate to other plots or stones? Is it located in the front of the cemetery, near the entrance? Is it in the back, near an area for maintenance? Is it in an area prone to flooding or sinking? The placement of a property is usually indicative of the amount spent on the plot, which ultimately connects to the power, prestige, or wealth of the deceased. Those who had a prominent place among the living have retained that position among the dead.
- *Size.* The size of the plot and monument are also usually strong indicators of the wealth of the deceased. Just as an item's cost often indicates its status value, it is reasonable to use material expenditure as a likely indicator of the prestige of the deceased.[6] The most visible cemetery expenditure is the private family mausoleum. The private family mausoleum became a popular form of memorialization for wealthy Americans, particularly industrial magnates, beginning in the late nineteenth century. These structures catch the visitor's eye due to their size, the amount of space they occupy, their landscaping, and their decoration—often including the family name, prominently displayed, and artistic embellishments such as bronze doors and stained glass windows. And while some mausoleums, in their standardization, betray their origins as catalogue models, others exhibit a great deal of artistic variation and detail. Indeed, such renowned American architects as Horace Trumbauer and Louis Sullivan included private family mausoleums among their commissions.

While most cemeteries have few (if any) private mausoleums, the size of other memorials can still be used to help determine an individual's status. Modern cemeteries frequently limit the size of a monument based upon the amount of grave space purchased. Purchasing a "single" grave might restrict the gravestone to a flush marker rather than an upright headstone. Cemetery rules and regulations usually impose size requirements or limitations for a stone or memorial, requiring a larger property for a larger memorial. In addition, "low-status" burials are more likely to be uniform in character, while the wealthy can afford monuments reflecting their individualism.[7]

Historical evaluations of monument size can be more difficult to make. While the rural cemetery movement began the move toward a cemetery "business" and established the use of rules and regulations, memorialization rules were not as they would become in modern cemeteries. As trends in cemetery design shifted, beginning in 1855 with the Landscape Lawn system developed by Adolph Strauch, priorities in monument design changed. Instead of the individual family plots crowded by monuments, cemeteries began to restrict monuments and prize open grassy areas. In spite of changes, however, material expenditure on memorialization can most often be correlated with the wealth of the deceased and used to orient a person's position within a community.

- *Composition of Materials.* The type of materials used in construction can also be used to assess the wealth and prestige of the deceased. Is the type of stone something that could have been obtained locally, or was it imported? Is it similar to the other monuments in the cemetery, or is it clearly made from a different type of stone? Is bronze or another valuable material used in the memorial?

- *Layout of the Plot.* With the establishment of Mount Auburn in 1831, many new shifts occurred in the ways Americans buried their dead. Among these changes was the concept of the family plot. For the first time, Americans would purchase a family plot, sometimes in advance of death, with the idea of future generations all being buried in one place together. Examining the arrangement of graves within a family's property, including the placement of those graves and the relationship of the graves to one another, can provide more clues about those buried there. *Who is centered on the property?* Often, the patriarch will center his grave in the middle of the plot and future generations will be buried radiating out from him. *Who is beside whom?* Within the family property, some burials may be set well apart from others. If you have access to cemetery records, you may be able to determine if there are any family members buried in the plot who don't have stones. In the case of a private family mausoleum, similar questions can be asked. *Who is buried outside of the mausoleum? Who is entombed in an eye-level crypt, and who is out of view at the top or bottom?* Analyzing a plot this way can help you determine family connections as well as positions of power within that family.

- *Content of Memorial.* The symbols and emblems on gravestones and other cemetery memorials point to the individual's interests while they were living. Among the most common emblems are religious symbols and iconography. Other icons pointing to aspects of an individual's life can be found through the clubs and fraternal organizations, occupations, flora/fauna, and designs depicted on their stones. Sometimes the shape of the stone itself is an indicator of the deceased's profession. Even after the establishment of the lawn park and the movement toward a more modern and commercial way of processing death and the dead, the bereaved could still make choices about their memorials, personalize or customize them, and apply their own meanings to the symbols.

- *Art and Architectural Styles.* Frequently, cemetery art and architecture reflects movements popular in the living community. Classical Revival, Egyptian Revival, Art Deco, Gothic Revival, Art Nouveau, and Beaux Arts are just some of the artistic styles found in cemeteries active in the past hundred years. Companies such as Tiffany Glass and Decorating published booklets criticizing the "commercial, crude, uninteresting" memorials in cemeteries, "completely devoid of all artistic merit,"[8] in an effort to convince Americans to purchase their own more "artistic" memorials. The choice of artistic style, while often grounded in popular trends, could also carry broader significance. For example, the popularity of Egyptian Revival style came in waves due to events in Egypt (Napoleon's entry into Egypt and, later, the discovery of King Tutankhamun's tomb). The Egyptians' fascination with and preparations for death made funerary art a popular way to express this style. Through obelisks, tomb construction, and Egyptian symbols, Egyptian Revival elements can be found in cemeteries across the country. Despite their popularity, however, these symbols also generated complaints (particularly in more religious communities) due to their origins. In this way, a person deciding to feature a sphinx, lotus flowers, or sun on his or her private mausoleum might have been influenced by the popular design of the day but also had a desire to show a more cosmopolitan worldview and a broader knowledge and appreciation for global art and events. These assumptions shouldn't be taken as absolutes in the absence of supporting evidence, but the artistic style of a memorial can provide priceless clues to the personality of the individual.

- *Epitaphs and Inscriptions.* The inscription on a gravestone can range from the simple and documentary (name or partial name) to the complex (lengthy description of life and achievements). Many people even select an inscription prior to death. An epitaph represents the self, projected onto a material object. It is thought and meant (by many) to last forever, and it can create the most lasting image of the deceased person. Analyzing inscriptions can tell us a great deal about the values and beliefs of the individual and his or her society. When we visit a cemetery and read the names on the stones, we construct an image of the deceased. Epitaphs can reveal when the deceased lived and died, what religion they subscribed to, their ethnicity, their place of birth, and sometimes what caused their death. For men (historically more often than women), epitaphs can record their profession, military campaigns, and achievements.

While name and life dates are the most common types of inscriptions, Americans have and continue to use epitaphs to communicate information about the deceased, including elements of their personality.[9] Sometimes even a short phrase is sufficient to conjure an image of the deceased. In West Laurel Hill Cemetery, the inscription "Cocktails at Six" catches the eye of visitors walking or driving by. The epitaph immediately conjures an image of a couple that liked to socialize, perhaps with daily drinks. Perhaps they were known for their cocktail hours or frequently said this phrase to friends and family. "Cocktails at Six" sounds like an invitation and acts as a happy thought of what the couple was doing in a perceived afterlife. That this inscription was completed "preneed," or in advance of death, tells the visitor that the couple wanted to create a distinct impression for future generations.

With the establishment of the "modern" cemetery and the movement toward a more commercial industry, gravestones and epitaphs were increasingly selected from sales books and catalogues. Even Sears, Roebuck & Co., and later Montgomery Ward, would sell cemetery monuments by catalogue. Consumers were still making choices, reflecting their beliefs and values, using additional customization of the stone or landscape to create a more personal element to the memorial. Clients who could afford monuments differing from the traditional stock offerings of catalogues purchased more individualized markers. This led to the "fashionable" cemeteries acquiring a much more diverse collection of designs.[10]

Documenting Stones: Questions to Ask and Record

Systematically recording inscriptions allows you to understand both the cemetery and the larger living community it served. Below is a list of questions to consider when analyzing gravestones.

1. What do the inscriptions used to describe women tell you about their roles in society? Does the word *relict* (widow) appear anywhere

in the cemetery? Are there any women who are described with attributes or roles other than *wife* or *mother*?

2. Is there any evidence of an epidemic passing through the community, or any natural disaster that struck? Examine whether the cause of death was recorded on the stone or whether an unusually high number of deaths occurred in a particular date range. What causes of death have been documented in the cemetery, and does that fit with what you know of the population living in the area at the time?

3. How many countries of origin are documented in the cemetery? Is there evidence of immigration and ethnic background in the symbolism or languages found on the stones? Are there any foreign languages used on cemetery markers?

4. Many larger cemeteries have sections (either officially designated or created by the lot owners themselves) for members of one ethnicity. Often purchased by a local association and then designated to members of the group, these areas are ways for an organization's members to be united in their place of burial, carrying their identification with a synagogue, church, or ethnic association through to death. Are there any sections in the cemetery (whether formal or informal) of predominantly one ethnicity? As cemeteries in America become "venues for religious practices and folk customs brought from foreign lands,"[11] the stones and memorials in these cemeteries often show evidence of ethnic identity. Do any such markers exist in your cemetery? Can you notice trends or differences in memorialization among different ethnic groups buried in the cemetery?

5. Is there any evidence of a change in the spelling of a last name over time? Whether due to a family rift or an effort to assimilate, descendants sometimes consciously choose to alter their last name. Make note of any discrepancies in spelling you find among family stones.

6. What religions are represented in the cemetery? What do the images and epitaphs tell you about how the deceased and their survivors felt about death and the afterlife? What words or phrases are associated with the concept of a spiritual afterlife?

7. What veterans are buried in the cemetery, and how are veterans' graves noted? Which wars or military branch did they serve in? Is there evidence of battles fought, or awards or ranks achieved?

8. What evidence is there of the occupations or trades people practiced in this community? Is there a great deal of diversity, or was the community based largely upon one industry?

9. What is the oldest date on a marker? What was the most recent burial?

10. Just as in the living community, cemeteries often feature organizational plots. Are there any of these "communities" of clubs, fraternal organizations, ethnic associations, or professional organizations? Are there plots purchased by an institution, such as a mental hospital, orphanage, or old age home? Within such plots, is there a single monument, or do members have individual markers? How do these monuments connect to one another and relate to the larger cemetery community?

11. Is there evidence of folk art or a local carver, or are the monuments uniform and mass-produced?

12. If it is possible to quantify the number of infants and small children buried within the cemetery, what time periods had the highest infant mortality rates? What kinds of symbols and phrases are found on the graves of children, and how do these differ from adult graves?

13. Are there any commemorative memorials to an entire group of people? Many of these monuments were erected with the intention of communicating "the memory or the ideals" of a local and national leader or culturally important individuals.[12] How does the memorial represent the ideals or values of those who erected it?

14. A cenotaph is a symbolic monument or inscription commemorating someone buried elsewhere or someone whose body was never recovered. Cenotaphs honor the dead even when their bodies are not present. Can you determine if there are cenotaphs present in the cemetery? Are they noted in a special monument or place in the cemetery? What does their designation say about their place among the community?

15. The typical, nondenominational American cemetery is largely made up of individual family plots with organizational plots interspersed throughout. An interesting aspect of the American cemetery is the way in which nonfamilial connections can be retained in death. In addition to organizational plots, in a modern cemetery you can frequently find the graves of business partners sitting side by side. Do you find any instances of business partners with adjoining plots?

16. Examine grave decorations (if any are present). What clues do they provide to the personality and interests of the deceased? Can you tell which parts of the cemetery are the most "active" by examining the prevalence of grave decorations?

Exercise: Using One Headstone to Open a Door to the Past

Just as headstones can be a source of biographical information for tour developers, the process of using one monument to inspire discussion can become an exercise or classroom project for students. Since many states have a local history education requirement, cemeteries across the country are being used to help fulfill that requirement, and sometimes it only takes one individual gravestone to illuminate several aspects of a community's history. Use figure 2.2 as an example.

This photograph of Frederick Faber's headstone was taken inside Marietta Cemetery in Marietta, Pennsylvania. Marietta is located in Lancaster County, a county settled in the early part of the eighteenth century. The town of Marietta, located along the Susquehanna River, became a lumber and iron-smelting center in the nineteenth century. This one gravestone inspires a number of questions and discussion points.

- The stone notes the date and place of the birth of Frederick Faber as 1812 in Germany. How does this reconcile with what is known about the ethnicity and immigration patterns in the area? Is there evidence of German ancestry present on other stones in this cemetery? Are there any other ethnic groups noted nearby in the cemetery?

- What can we tell about Frederick Faber's family from examining the cemetery? Is there any evidence of other stones or inscriptions nearby with the same surname? What is the significance that this is the only visible stone still upright in the area? Is there anything noteworthy about its relationship to other stones in the cemetery (on a hill, isolated, near a prominent place, etc.)?

- Does Frederick Faber's stone match the others in the cemetery in terms of size, type, material level of decoration, and style of lettering? Is it more ornate, more simple, or does it fit in with the other stones in the cemetery community?

- In addition to "In memory of," there is a description of the cause of death noted on this stone as well as the deceased's employer and location of death. What does this tell you about the working conditions for immigrants working in the Marietta Furnace? Why do you think the survivors recorded his death in this way? Why do you think they would have chosen this as an inscription rather than listing surviving family members or a religious verse or symbol? How does Faber's life become defined by his death? How do you think others

Figure 2.2.　Faber Monument, Marietta, Pennsylvania.
Photograph by author.

reacted to seeing this stone following his death? In an era before active labor unions and OSHA (the Occupational Safety and Health Act), workers had little recourse in the event of workplace injury or death. Do you think this was a way for his family to protest the way he died or merely an objective record of the facts?

For teachers, a lesson plan starting with a cemetery stone can also become an exercise for students to use other primary and secondary sources to augment the information found on the stone and to create a fuller picture of the deceased.

- Does the town of Marietta have a historical society or library that might retain newspaper clippings on the accident?
- Does the Marietta Furnace survive in some way, and do its records exist? Are there photographs of the furnace?
- Are there books that talk about mid-nineteenth-century Pennsylvania iron furnaces and the conditions experienced while working for one?
- Are there any diaries, letters, or other documents written by workers from the furnace or members of the community of Marietta in the mid-nineteenth century? How do they describe life during this time?
- Does the cemetery retain records showing if anyone else is buried with Frederick Faber?
- Do census records show where he lived, who he lived with, and when he came to America?
- Does a local phone book show anyone with that same surname living in Marietta today?

A stone such as this one certainly conveys an element of local history, but it could also be used in teaching broader lessons on immigration and industrial development and working conditions.

Research: Art and Design Elements

Just as a survey of a cemetery's gravestones is essential when determining *who* is buried within a cemetery, a site survey is also a vital part of determining what art and design elements are present. These can later help with creating fuller cemetery programming. Consult Appendix A for state-by-state references, or see Appendix B for sources that can advise on how to conduct and complete a cemetery site evaluation and to create a cemetery site map. Among the physical elements a site map should include are buildings and structures, boundary lines, walks and pathways fences, gates, entrances, terraces, retaining walls, and the layout of graves.[13] If the cemetery has already been surveyed or evaluated, obtain a copy of the materials. Perhaps the cemetery was surveyed as part of a larger state or regional historic district. Any work that has already been done on the site is a starting place for evaluating gaps in information.

Once a survey has been conducted, look to other sources to augment the information collected. Bringing in experts in landscape design, masonry, and bronze and ironwork can illuminate aspects of the cemetery's construction. Examine maps and deeds to gather an understanding of what the land looked like prior to the cemetery, who purchased the land, and what was done to the site to transform it into a place for burials. Use local libraries, archives, and historical societies to look for photographs of what the cemetery once looked like, along with other archival sources documenting the founding and development of the cemetery. If your community has an institution that maintains architectural records, consult these for documents pertaining to cemetery development and the construction of significant buildings and monuments.

Depending upon the age and origins of the cemetery, the stones might have been constructed by local carvers, mass-produced by companies out of state and purchased through catalogues, or designed for each individual by a professional monument company.

1. *Stone Carvers.* If the marker was created by a stone carver, look for his name inscribed at the base of the stone in the back. Depending upon what geographical area the cemetery is located in, there could be a great deal of research about local stonecutters. (New England graveyards in particular have been heavily researched.) Consult the Association for Gravestone Studies (http://www.gravestonestudies. org) for resources on stone carvers from your geographic area.

2. *Granite and Monument Design Catalogues.* While the stones purchased through these catalogues might not have the most artistic merit, nor are they frequently the most personalized, they are able to provide information about the community the cemetery served by showing how people purchased monuments; what designs, epitaphs, and symbols they chose; and what they were spending on them. You can also tell to what degree customers chose personal customization over uniform, standard purchases. Some catalogues provide design hints, along with symbols and what they represent. Many of these granite and monument catalogues are available online through

websites such as http://www.quarriesandbeyond.org, and through
websites documenting the work of twentieth-century quarries.

3. *Trade Publications.* Late nineteenth- and early twentieth-century
trade publications such as *Monumental News* provide information
on cemetery trends and vendors from across the country. These
publications also featured the installation of particularly expensive
or noteworthy monuments and can be a source for tracking down
the architect, firm, or amount paid for a monument or mausoleum.

Research: Documenting the Natural Elements

Cemeteries and graveyards straddle natural space and urban development.
While the settlement of the land is reflected in the establishment of burial
grounds, sometimes these grounds were never fully developed or retained
significant green space. Over time, and particularly if not maintained, some
revert back to their more natural state. As the areas surrounding them
become more developed, perceptions are transformed and the cemetery
itself becomes seen as a "green" space. This natural environment can help
researchers understand the cemetery community and also provide material
for tours and programs. Cemeteries and organizations using cemeteries for
education are currently doing programs including the birds, trees, flow-
ering plants, bees, bats, butterflies, fireflies, dragonflies, mushrooms, and
even the rocks and minerals that are all part of the cemetery space. If they
have not been completed, conduct both a wildlife inventory and a natural
features inventory. Create a spreadsheet, and note the date and location of
any wildlife spotted. Ask staff, volunteers, and visitors to assist. While many
cemeteries consider natural wildlife as "pests," many others are working to
be good environmental stewards by creating and allowing animal habitats
on cemetery grounds. Some cemeteries hold events focused on viewing a
few species, such as "Mount Auburn's Nighthawks," which focuses on the
fall migration of the common nighthawk.

When inventorying the site's natural features, note the cemetery's orientation and the orientation of the graves. Are all graves oriented to the
same direction? How does the cemetery's physical placement relate to the
living community? What streams, ponds, or other water features are part
of the landscape? Are there any natural boundaries such as streams or cliffs?
Are there natural elements that led the founders to choose this location for
the cemetery, such as accessibility or natural vistas and scenic overlooks?

If necessary, bring in outside assistance (an arborist or horticulturalist)
to help identify the trees and plantings in the cemetery. Note whether

plantings are indigenous or were introduced to the area and purposefully planted in the space. Try to determine the age of the trees on site. Is there anything special cultivated in the cemetery? Try to determine the reasons for the introduced plantings. Plantings might have been placed in certain areas of the cemetery for aesthetic reasons. Flowerbeds and shade trees help to create a beautiful atmosphere of a peaceful rest. Sometimes certain types of plantings have utilitarian purposes, such as helping to prevent and control erosion. Plants and trees such as ivy and cypress can also have symbolic meanings. For some Christians, the dogwood flower acts as a symbol for the blood of Jesus on the cross, and daffodils and narcissus as flowers symbolizing resurrection, while some African Americans believe the use of thorny yucca and cactus help prevent the spirit's movement around the cemetery.[14] When conducting a survey, remember, plants that have taken over parts of the burial ground might have been deliberately planted as part of the historic design of the cemetery.

After researching the people, art and design, and natural elements of the cemetery, the next step is to organize your findings. When you are researching the dead buried in a cemetery, keep lists or create a database. Depending upon your resources, you may be looking to develop a single walking tour—or perhaps you'll develop a number of themed walking tours. Such themed tours can be developed around any group of people, not just famous names, or around any topic. You can keep lists of women, or members of a particular race or religion. Create lists based on professions, athletes, military veterans, or the infamous or philanthropic. Your database should pull all information together in one place, including the location of the deceased, the dates they lived, and anything notable about the memorial. Keeping a spreadsheet or database makes it easier not only to remember who you've researched but also to pull together content for specialty themed tours. Keep hard copies of materials for reference in the development of future programs. Make notes of which people or subject areas have been exhaustively documented and which still need to be researched.

Tour Development: Assembling Content and Themes, Creating a Tour and Executing

Step 1: Determining Content for a Walking Tour

One of the first of many factors to consider when developing content for a walking tour is audience. Will this tour be done in conjunction with a library, museum, or other historical institution? In conjunction with a festival, program, special event, or holiday? Is it for a school group? Veterans? Or are you just intending to develop a tour for the general public? Answering the audience question is important because it helps you tailor the tour to the interests of the group.

Prior to developing a themed or specialty tour, establishing a basic introduction or "101 Tour" is an essential way to introduce the public to the cemetery and to begin the process of getting them acclimated to cemetery programming. In addition to its benefits for the public, the 101 Tour can help you (and your colleagues) become more comfortable developing tours, giving tours, and teaching others to give tours. It is the foundation upon which other cemetery tours can be built. The content you develop in preparing this tour can help fill in future themed tours. A 101 Tour should be broad enough to appeal to most audiences; it should be viewed as an introduction to the cemetery, not an in-depth study. Although it is not a themed tour per se, there should be some general principles or objectives guiding its creation. Perhaps the cemetery is known for one particular monument, design element, or person. Whether your goal is to discuss local interest stories, emphasize the diversity in monument styles or people buried the cemetery, focus on the art and symbols on the stones themselves, or some combination of the above, understanding and communicating your goals will help prevent the tour from becoming a walk interspersed with a random jumble of facts.

Following the successful creation of an introductory cemetery tour, look to a variety of different sources for inspiration for themed tours. Tours can connect the deceased in any number of imaginable ways. Cemeteries are unique venues where nature, material culture, art, history, symbolism, death, and societal views of death all collide, creating countless opportunities for discussion and programs. If you are thinking about creating a cemetery tour, a simple way to find inspiration is to subscribe to the newsletters of cemeteries already conducting cemetery tours (see the end of this chapter for select examples). Use other cemeteries for inspiration, but then transform these ideas to fit your cemetery. For example, some popular cemetery tours center on former beer brewers, but not every cemetery has beer barons among its dead, nor is every cemetery open to allowing alcohol-themed events. Instead, a tour of Prohibition activists might be a better fit! Stay tuned in to your community. Be aware of upcoming anniversaries, events, and special exhibitions, and try to partner with community organizations to create timely tours. Cemeteries are full of local interest stories and "undiscovered" history.

The challenge is to tap in to what the community is interested in hearing about. Ask lot owners or members of a friends group what kind of tour they would like to see.

An important consideration is to have an arc to the story. To avoid a disjointed and disconnected tour, think first about a comprehensive theme. Often the best tour or cemetery program begins not with a list of who is buried there, but a great idea or something timely and interesting that will engage visitors. Maybe you've developed a concept or story you'd like to tell. You might know of one or two anchor names that connect directly, but research can then be done to fill in the gaps. While the individuals buried in your cemetery might appear to have little connection to one another, think about the reasons they were buried in one place and the things they had in common, and how these lives fit together to tell an overall story.

Even after developing a basic introductory tour, be aware of and open to the idea that new research can and will change the narrative. Be open to scholars and researchers bringing additional information to light. Once a cemetery opens itself to public tours, more interest generated will result in new lives being illuminated. And while the dead may not change, our interpretation of their lives does. We can revisit someone's life as new information is uncovered or as current events shape our perception of the past. The content is timeless yet current, and it can always be remixed and reinterpreted to reach new audiences.

Step 2: Assemble the Content for the Tour

Once you have decided on a theme and constructed the storyline, assemble the following materials:

- *The Basic Facts.* Create a fact sheet with as many of the following questions answered as you can: (1) What year was the cemetery founded? (2) Who were the founders, and why did they choose to start this cemetery? (3) Where was the community burying its dead prior to this cemetery's founding? (4) Who designed the cemetery, and how was it originally laid out? (5) How does this cemetery compare to other local or regional burial grounds? (6) How many acres does it cover? (7) What is the oldest section, and how did the grounds expand over time? (8) How did funeral processions originally travel here? (9) Are there still burials occurring? If so, how many per year? (10) How many people are buried in the cemetery? (11) How many monuments are there in the cemetery? (12) Are there still plots for sale? (13) Who owns the cemetery now, and who is responsible for maintenance?

- *A Map of the Cemetery.* A map of the cemetery should show roads, paths, entrances, and major landmarks and buildings. A more detailed map is better for locating graves; however, if one does not exist, use whatever map is available. Even in small cemeteries, a notable marker, epitaph, or person might never be found again without a map and numbering system.

- *The People.* Create a list of the names and burial locations of all of the deceased who are possible candidates for inclusion on the tour. For an introductory tour, think about who the well-known deceased are, but avoid including only members of one group (rich white men) in favor of including a wider representation of the burials in the cemetery. Consider including not just well-known names or town founders but a cross section of people whose lives shaped the living community. Include stops where there is a funny or memorable story. Not every stop has to be of profound historical importance. You want the tour to be memorable as well. Write short biographies for all of the individuals whose graves you might want to visit, noting how their stories relate to the theme of the tour—or, for a 101 Tour, noting why you think they should be a part of a fundamental cemetery tour. Try to put their stories into context. Although it is unlikely that everyone on your initial list will make the cut, the more information you assemble, the better. Once you've drawn up a comprehensive list, you can begin to make choices, noting key figures or stops that you feel are essential to the story.

- *Landmarks.* Create a list of monuments, memorials, and landmarks (both natural and constructed). Cemetery landmarks can include a gate or main entrance, gatehouse, chapel, bell tower, or community monument. If there are gravestones or memorials designed by a notable stone carver or architect, include them. An introductory tour can be very subjective. If there is a stone or inscription that has caught your eye, include it on the list, along with any known information such as the material it was made from or how much the property or memorial was purchased for. Think about what this cemetery has that others don't—whether it's a collection of a certain type of marker, work by a local stone cutter, an ethnic section with distinct memorialization, or a mausoleum designed by a famous architect. Your list of landmarks should include dates of construction (if known) along with the architect and/or artist who designed them.

- *Types of Monuments.* Particularly for an introductory tour, it is helpful to point out monument types. For example, the obelisk is a common nineteenth-century cemetery monument type. Visitors might be familiar with the shape but not know its name, its origins, or the symbolism behind it. Be aware of both the common and most unusual types of monuments in the cemetery and what their origins are.
- *Common Symbols.* Create a catalogue of cemetery symbols. As you are stopping at individual graves, point out symbolic carvings on the gravestone or on the monuments nearby.
- *Natural Elements.* Note any natural elements visitors might be interested in. If the cemetery has any award-winning or notable trees, include a note about them. If there is a planting unique to the area or something few other cemeteries have, point that out. Explain the meaning behind any symbolic plantings.
- *Superlatives.* Superlatives can act as "fun facts," as Americans are frequently interested in the biggest, first, or most expensive. If you have access to this information, create a list of the tallest memorial, the most expensive memorial, the first burial, and the biggest family plot.

Step 3: Constructing the Tour

Although gathering information for your tour can be difficult, winnowing it down can be even more of a challenge. Three primary factors should guide your choices: the tour's theme; which stops fit best within that theme; and whether these stops will fit along the route of the tour.

- *Mapping the Route.* In many ways, mapping the route is the most important part of the process of creating a cemetery tour. It is essential to figure out how far it is to a certain site and how long it will take to get there. Consider whether the walk is uphill or over uneven terrain. Placing all of the tour-stop candidates on a map will help you visualize the location of any outliers—but only by walking from stop to stop will you be able to ascertain the physical toll of the trek. Your typical cemetery tour should last no more than two hours and should not require too much strenuous walking. If the cemetery is large, it's unlikely that your tour will cover the entire grounds—and some stops may need to be excluded simply because of the distance they'd add to the route.
- *Time on the Ground.* Spending time walking the cemetery is a vital part of preparation for a tour. It enables you to find the best and easiest

route from point to point. The more time you spend familiarizing yourself with markers and landmarks, the easier it will be to find those stops while leading a walking tour. As you walk the route, examine what you pass along the way. There might be an opportunity to point out a gravestone you might not normally notice. Try to think of the tour from the point of view of visitors and anticipate what might catch their eyes when walking the route for the first time. Think about what people will likely ask about, and be prepared to answer.

Step 4: Prior to the Tour

- *Practice!* Practice not just the script but also finding the locations for the burials. While maps may be useful for providing a big-picture overview of the tour stops, on the ground you have a different visual experience. Take a map on your practice run. If necessary, physically mark the ground at any places that will remind you when to turn off the path and into the section where the grave is located. Simple marking flags can be purchased inexpensively at hardware stores and can be important guides when looking for a grave. If you are confident that you can lead the tour without a map or marking flags, use trees or other monuments or indicators to guide your way.
- *Create Visuals.* Walking tours can be enhanced by the simple act of including visuals: a photograph of the deceased or their home or business can make a lasting impression, particularly if the home or business still stands in the community. Create color photocopies of these images and laminate them to prevent weather damage from unexpected weather. Tactile objects and audio equipment also help create a multidimensional portrait of the deceased, although carrying such materials can become cumbersome. Fortunately, in the digital era, something as small as an iPhone can be used to show images or play music related to the deceased, and is easy to carry in a back pocket.
- *Reminders to Participants.* If you are able to contact members of the group before the tour, remind them to wear comfortable shoes and to bring bug spray, sunscreen, water, or an umbrella or appropriate gear if inclement weather is expected.

Step 5: Starting the Tour

- *Introduction.* Welcome the group. Introduce yourself and the organization you are representing (whether it's the cemetery or an outside organization). If you are employed by the cemetery or are part of a friends group, explain your mission and why you are conducting cemetery tours. If you are part of an outside group or organization, explain what made you decide to use the cemetery as an education tool. The introduction is an important opportunity to explain the concept of cemetery tours as preservation. You can allay fears of disrespecting the dead by explaining the ways in which the tour will help preserve the cemetery. Consider mentioning why you chose to be a guide in a cemetery, and what initially drew you there.

- *Safety Warning.* Provide a safety warning. Even the most well-maintained cemeteries have holes and uneven surfaces or sunken areas. Whether you are spending most of the time on the paths or on grass, warn visitors of the uneven terrain. Also request that visitors refrain from leaning or standing on the memorials.
- *General Information.* Include a mention of the location of restrooms (if there are any), as well as a request to mute cell phones and a request to be respectful if mourners are present.
- *Site Background, History, and Chronology.* Before starting the tour, give a brief overview of how the cemetery was founded. Why? By whom? How does it compare to other local cemeteries in terms of its age? Is it a special type of cemetery, or does it represent a certain style? Any significance as to how it was laid out? When was it most active? If burials are still occurring, mention that too. Was there anything significant about why it was founded? How does it fit in with broader cemetery trends across the nation? Be sure to mention if the cemetery has a special designation (such as inclusion on the national or regional register of historic places). While not all of these items need to be addressed in the opening of the tour, it is useful to have the content available to interject between stops if necessary, or if visitors ask.

Step 6: Conducting the Tour

- Once you have started the tour, move from site to site as promptly as possible, but wait until the entire group has assembled before talking about the stop.
- Use notes if necessary, but avoid reading from a script.

Step 7: Concluding the Tour

- Thank the group for attending!
- One of the primary objectives of any cemetery tour is to entice the public to care enough to return to the cemetery, whether for

a formal event or on their own. Let them know about upcoming events and tours. If the tour was sponsored by a friends group or nonprofit organization, mention membership. If the cemetery or organization supporting the cemetery is accepting volunteers, make tour participants aware of those opportunities.

- Invite participants to take a tour survey. Hand out brief surveys or direct them to an online survey.

Tips, Troubles, and Suggestions

- *What if no map exists?* It is extremely difficult, even in the smallest burial ground, to comprehensively survey and maintain a grasp on the content of the cemetery without a map to orient you. There are several outstanding resources available to help guide you in the process of creating a map if none exists (see Appendix B).
- *How do I avoid getting lost?* Even the most experienced guide can get turned around among the thousands of stones in some of the larger cemeteries. It is essential for you to practice the route, make notes of stopping points, pay attention to those markers, and not hesitate to use marking flags to highlight a hard-to-find grave.
- *What if the deceased on the tour has no gravestone or marker?* Even in the wealthiest cemeteries, countless individuals lie in unmarked graves. Perhaps a stone was never constructed, or maybe it fell over at some point and was buried (a common practice in some cemeteries). Perhaps it has become so worn or broken that you can no longer identify it. Or, as is sometimes the case in historic rural cemeteries, the mausoleum is *underground* with no visible construction above the surface. Try to determine if a marker was ever installed on the site by checking archival records (either the cemetery's records or probate records from the deceased's estate). A probe of the plot, to be conducted only with the express permission of the cemetery ownership, can sometimes indicate if a marker was buried. Try to approximate the location of the burial by noting the location of neighboring graves and/or the boundaries of the family plot. If you can pinpoint the exact gravesite, use a temporary marker to indicate the space to tour participants. In instances in which there is no marker and no way of determining the exact location of the grave, it's even more helpful to provide an image connected with the deceased.

- *What if a key person for my tour is buried too far out of the way to incorporate?* Sometimes a burial site is just too far out of reach to make the trek to the grave. There are three options in this instance. One, you could orient the tour from another point in the cemetery (start at another entrance or use another point as a springboard). Two, if you have enough content, you could break the tour into a two-part series, each covering a different part of the cemetery. Or, three, you could stop and point in the direction of the person's burial site, mention why he or she is important, and offer to provide directions to the gravesite after the tour is over. Unfortunately, in larger cemeteries it is not always possible to reach every destination on one tour.

The following are tips to keep in mind:

- If you can connect the name of the deceased with a school, park, or street in the community, it makes the story more memorable and reminds your audience of the historical underpinnings of everyday life.
- Particularly in a cemetery still actively burying people, try to learn at least a small amount about the burial process. People will ask! Even though they might be apprehensive, the public is often curious about burials. Ask a superintendent, sexton, or caretaker the basics of burial depths, vaults, and digging a grave.
- Have some basic knowledge of the memorial materials used in your cemetery. Be able to tell the difference between marble, granite, or whatever materials comprise the majority of markers. Know where these materials came from and how they got to the cemetery.
- Watch the time! Try not to linger on any one stop for too long. A good length for a cemetery tour is under two hours, and you don't want to have to move at an uncomfortable rate to keep the group on time. Unlike in a museum or historical site where a visitor usually can voluntarily leave the tour, once on the cemetery grounds it might be difficult for audience members to find their way back to the entrance. Staying on time reduces the likelihood that someone will want to try to leave the tour early.
- Watch your pace. Practice runs will help you grasp how many stops you can make in the allotted time and how long you can stay at each stop. Choose a brisk pace, but not one that will exhaust participants or cause slower walkers to fall behind. Build in extra time in case the group has slower walkers or asks a lot of questions.

- When possible, stay on the paths. Choose terrain that is less steep and easier to traverse. If you are able to control when the grass is cut, try to keep the maintenance as regular as possible along the tour route.
- Carry a cell phone. Cemeteries can be large, isolated, and isolating spaces. If an emergency occurs along the route or someone twists an ankle, it is essential to be able to reach help.
- Be careful not to lose anyone. Be sure to get an accurate count of participants before your tour sets out, and wrangle people to keep them with the group. Visitors can get easily distracted by other monuments or gravesites. Sometimes there are participants who hope to slink away from the group in order to be able to spend the night in a cemetery alone. Counting the group a couple of times along the way and keeping an eye out for stragglers helps prevent losing a member during the tour.
- Be ready for inclement weather. One of the most difficult variables to manage is the weather. Inform tour participants in advance whether the tour will proceed in light rain or be rescheduled.
- Have an escape route! Prepare in advance for what you'll do if you have to cut the tour short due to extreme weather, time constraints, or the physical condition of the group. Know an easy way to get back to the start from any point along the tour route.
- If the cemetery you are using for your tour is still "active" and conducting burials, check the burial schedule prior to the date of the tour. Understand that you might have to alter your route due to a burial or the presence of mourners nearby, and plan accordingly.
- Point out sites with a broad appeal even if they don't necessarily fit with the theme of the tour. A disaster like the sinking of the *Titanic* is a well-known tragedy that continues to generate a great amount of popular interest. If you are giving a tour and pass by the memorial of a *Titanic* survivor, it's an item of interest that is likely to stay in the mind of the tour participants.
- Know a little about a lot. While a cemetery guide should certainly be familiar with the content of the tour he or she is leading, having a little bit of knowledge about other aspects of the cemetery (the trees, sculpture, and art) lends a broader base of knowledge to the tour. The more time you spend in the cemetery, the more you will know where your "favorites" are. You might not be an arborist, but pointing out your favorite tree and what you like about it might enable you to connect with someone on the tour. The audience can also read your love and enthusiasm for the cemetery, and maybe some of that can be transferred to them.

- If you don't know the answer to a question, don't make something up!
- Be prepared for ghost questions. Cemetery visitors often like a good ghost story or want to know if the cemetery is "haunted," but just as many people could be alienated by talk of spirits and ghosts. Knowing and reading the audience can help you determine how to address ghost questions.

Communication Tips

The beauty of the cemetery and the interesting lives of the cemetery residents are only two of the ingredients in creating a successful cemetery tour. "Strong content must be matched with a strong presentation."[15] An engaging and knowledgeable guide becomes a tremendous ambassador for the cemetery, and his or her knowledge and enthusiasm can make a powerful impact on an audience.

- *Speaking and Volume.* A tour guide, regardless of the locale, should always strive to speak clearly and articulately. However, giving a tour outside adds a new dimension to public speaking. A cemetery tour guide might have to contend with noise created by traffic, wind, overhead airplanes, and lawnmowers. If your tour group contains more than twenty people, a portable microphone should be used. In addition, before you start speaking, wait for the entire group to gather, and make eye contact with everyone to confirm that they are ready to listen. Use the natural terrain of the cemetery to help project your voice; elevating yourself above the crowd by standing on a hill, incline, or steps will help your voice to carry.
- *Eye Contact and Body Language.* Maintain good eye contact with the audience, and try not to fidget.
- *Be Sensitive.* Cemeteries are emotionally laden places for many people. They may fear them or dread visiting. Perhaps a tour participant is visiting the cemetery for the first time following the loss of a loved one. People who regularly spend time in cemeteries sometimes forget that not everyone is comfortable wandering around in the land of the dead. Be mindful and respectful of the varied perspectives your tour participants are likely to have.
- *Avoid Euphemisms, Slang, and Jargon.* Avoid words like *cremains* (a slang term for cremated remains), euphemisms like *bit the dust*, and jargon (words only cemetery or funeral professionals would know). Visitors might find slang terms and euphemisms to be disrespectful

and unprofessional, while esoteric terms might alienate those not part of the in group. Use accessible language, and don't hesitate to explain if someone doesn't understand a term.

- *Read the Crowd.* Pay attention to the group to see if they are engaged. Be open and flexible to questions, and don't force your agenda upon them. If you have the sense the group is more interested in one subject than another, try to adjust the content of the tour to fit their interests.
- *Interaction.* When possible, try to make the tour interactive by phrasing some of the content as questions and asking for a "show of hands" in response. Groups will often respond better to a conversational presentation than they will to a straight lecture.
- *Cultural Connections.* Try to make connections that will relate to the group. For example, Dave Horwitz, a long-time Laurel Hill Cemetery tour guide, likes to point out the grave of Robert Cornelius when he has a teenage school group. Why? Cornelius took the world's first "selfie" back in 1839, three years after the founding of Laurel Hill. A selfie is something most (if not all) of the teenagers in his tour group have taken, and pointing out Cornelius (along with showing his "selfie") creates a way for them to relate to someone who lived more than 175 years ago.
- *Other Tours.* Attend other tours, particularly cemetery tours, to learn from other guides. Every guide has different strengths, styles, and approaches. Learn and adapt your presentation based upon what you see from others.

Standardizing the Message and Developing Guide Training

It is important to formalize and standardize the tour process for several reasons. From the cemetery's perspective, controlling the message becomes a vital part of marketing and building awareness. Being formal and deliberate about the tour process leads both to better tours and better guides, both of which will increase the likelihood that visitors will want to return.

- *Improve the "101 Tour."* Learn from this foundation when building other themed tours.
- *Debrief after each tour.* This should be done whether by surveying the participants or gauging your own impressions. Consider the subject of the tour, the content, the delivery, and the guide's general knowledge

base and performance. Note the reception the tour received and any ways to improve going forward.

- *Research.* Develop a database of scripts with references to the accompanying research. Develop a history or vetting committee to review scripts and to check for accuracy. Have a process in place for disseminating new information and updating scripts as new information is uncovered.
- *Formalize the Script Development Process.* Use approved scripts, and avoid passing along anecdotes that can't be substantiated.
- *Develop a Tour Checklist.* This should include items to be touched on in an introduction, as well as basic facts to be addressed either at the beginning of the tour or at some point along the route. Include key figures along with optional names and markers to fit in if time allows. Also include fun "superlatives," such as the tallest or biggest monuments, largest plots, and firsts, such as the first burial or first section created.
- *Develop a Formal Training Program for New Guides.* Most cemeteries conducting robust tour schedules have a formal guide-training process. They may refer to it as docent training, guide training, or, in the case of Elmwood Cemetery in Memphis, Tennessee, "Ambassador College," but these training programs have common goals. They are looking to create qualified guides to help manage the increased demand for both public and private tours, along with maintaining control over the messages they are communicating to visitors. While the training varies in each organization, there are some core components to each. First, cemeteries usually have required reading on the history and general facts of the cemetery and the people buried there. They also want guides to be familiar with the cemetery's mission and vision. Second, they require attendance at existing tours and then have new guides pair up with and shadow existing guides. After attending the necessary tours and training sessions, guide candidates do a practice run with a current guide. As part of the training, "continuing education sessions" on special topics such as researching for cemetery tours, effective communication, cemetery symbolism, and basics of monuments and burials help to give the guide access to even more helpful information. When they are prepared to lead their own tour, they usually have criteria to meet to successfully pass the training and to lead tours on their own. Often they are required to begin with an established general orientation tour before moving to more esoteric topics. The result of this process is not just a higher quality of tour but also better representatives and ambassadors for the cemetery.

Tours and Types

The diversity in cemetery walking tours currently being offered in cemeteries around the country is striking. Whether it's a nature-based tour, a tour focusing on the art and architecture in the cemetery, or a tour based upon one person, cemetery programmers are creating new ways to use the cemetery to educate visitors. The following is a list of a few of the cemetery tours occurring across the country.

Tours Based around One Person

Sometimes one person's story can develop into a walking tour with several different stops.

Some examples are:

- "Emily McDonnell: A Monumental Woman" (Forest Lawn, Buffalo, New York; McDonnell was an executive of a monument firm whose work can be found in the cemetery)
- "Mark Twain's Companions and Cohorts" (Cedar Hill Cemetery, Hartford, Connecticut)
- "Dillinger and the Eastside Notables" (Crown Hill Cemetery, Indianapolis, Indiana)

Local Interest

- "Hartford Landmarks and Legacies" (Cedar Hill Cemetery, Hartford, Connecticut)
- "Rochester and the Legendary Eric Canal" (Mount Hope Cemetery, Rochester, New York)
- "The Deering Neighborhood: People and Places" (Evergreen Cemetery, Portland, Maine)
- "Always on Tap: A History of Philadelphia's Water System" (Laurel Hill Cemetery, Philadelphia, Pennsylvania)
- "All Dressed up and Six Feet Below: The Movers and Shakers of Old Philadelphia" (Laurel Hill Cemetery, Philadelphia, Pennsylvania)

Work and Commerce

- "Seafaring Portlanders" (Evergreen Cemetery, Portland, Maine)
- "A Cure for What Ails You: A History of Medical Men and Women in Philadelphia" (Laurel Hill Cemetery, Philadelphia, Pennsylvania)

- "Malts and Vaults: Where Beer Meets History" (Historic Oakland Cemetery, Atlanta, Georgia)

One Event

- "Buffalo Electrified" (Forest Lawn Cemetery, Buffalo, New York; commemorating the 1901 Pan American Exposition)
- "The Portland Rum Riot" (Evergreen Cemetery, Portland, Maine)
- "1876: The Centennial and the Cemetery" (Laurel Hill Cemetery, Philadelphia, Pennsylvania)
- "Fear and Accusation: The Leo Frank Story" (Historic Oakland Cemetery, Atlanta, Georgia)
- "Flu Epidemic of 1918" (Crown Hill Cemetery, Indianapolis, Indiana)

Wars, Veterans, and the Military

- "From Homefires to Campfires: Hartford Women and the Civil War" (Cedar Hill Cemetery, Hartford, Connecticut)
- "The Spanish American War" (Evergreen Cemetery, Portland, Maine)
- "War of 1812: The Battle of Plattsburgh" (Oakwood Cemetery, Troy, New York)

Art and Design

- "Monumental Design: Lettering in Green-Wood" (Green-Wood Cemetery, Brooklyn, New York)
- "Form, Function, and Mount Hope Cemetery" (Mount Hope Cemetery, Rochester, New York; focusing on design elements within the cemetery)
- "Green-Wood House Tour" (Green-Wood Cemetery, Brooklyn, New York; a look inside private family mausoleums)
- "Monuments, Memory, and the Cultural Landscape" (Evergreen Cemetery, Portland, Maine; a discussion of forms, types of materials, symbolism, and landscape of the cemetery)
- "Ironworking" (Oakwood Cemetery, Troy, New York; a tour of the cemetery's ornamental ironwork)
- "What's Inside There? Family Mausoleums" (Oakwood Cemetery, Troy, New York)

- "Celtic Crosses Tour" (Oakwood Cemetery, Troy, New York)
- "Epitaphs—The Immortality of Words" (Historic Oakland Cemetery, Atlanta, Georgia)
- "Having the Last Word: Epitaphs and Grave Writings of Laurel Hill" (Laurel Hill Cemetery, Philadelphia, Pennsylvania)

Nature

- "Finding Fungi" (Oakwood Cemetery, Troy, New York)
- "Biodiversity at Mount Auburn" (Mount Auburn Cemetery, Cambridge, Massachusetts; looking for evidence of reptiles and amphibians as part of Mount Auburn's Wildlife Action Plan)
- "Firefly Night: Nature Nights at the Woodlands" (The Woodlands, Philadelphia, Pennsylvania)

Race and Ethnicity

- "From *Amistad* to *Brown v. Board of Ed*: Mount Auburn's Supreme Court Justices and Civil Rights Cases" (Mount Auburn Cemetery, Cambridge, Massachusetts)
- "Of Blessed Memory: Jewish Notables of Laurel Hill Cemetery" (Laurel Hill Cemetery, Philadelphia, Pennsylvania)
- "Juneteenth—A Walking Tour" (Mount Auburn Cemetery, Cambridge, Massachusetts)

Miscellaneous

- "Gay Green-Wood" (Green-Wood Cemetery, Brooklyn, New York; an LGBT tour for Pride Week)
- "Crooked Cronies: Philadelphia's Profiteering Politicians of the Past" (Laurel Hill Cemetery, Philadelphia, Pennsylvania)
- "Transplanted Souls: Another Try at Eternal Rest" (Laurel Hill Cemetery, Philadelphia, Pennsylvania)
- "Bandmasters, Fifers, Composers, and More: Oakland's Music Makers (Historic Oakland Cemetery, Atlanta, Georgia)
- "From Able-Bodied to Disembodied: Laurel Hill's Athletes" (Laurel Hill Cemetery, Philadelphia, Pennsylvania)
- "Philanthropic Philadelphians: In the Spirit of Thanks and Giving" (Laurel Hill Cemetery, Philadelphia, Pennsylvania)

- "Love on the Rocks: Love Stories" (Historic Oakwood Cemetery, Raleigh, North Carolina)
- "Classy Broads and Daring Dames: The Ladies of Laurel Hill" (Laurel Hill Cemetery, Philadelphia, Pennsylvania)
- "Cranks, Catalysts, and Collisions" (Mount Hope Cemetery, Rochester, New York; nonfamous names who had an impact on famous events)
- "Odd Fellows, Red Men, Masons and More . . . Fraternal Organizations at Oakland" (Historic Oakland Cemetery, Atlanta, Georgia)
- "Butler University Notables at Crown Hill" (Crown Hill Cemetery, Indianapolis, Indiana)
- "Indianapolis Auto Greats" (Crown Hill Cemetery, Indianapolis, Indiana)
- "Yellow Fever: A Tour of the Plague" (Elmwood Cemetery, Memphis, Tennessee)
- "Scandals and Scoundrels" (Elmwood Cemetery, Memphis, Tennessee)
- "The Memphis Music Tour: A Walking Tour through Elmwood" (Elmwood Cemetery, Memphis, Tennessee)
- "What a Way to Go!" (Cedar Hill Cemetery, Hartford, Connecticut)
- "Spirits and Spiritualists" (Laurel Hill Cemetery, Philadelphia, Pennsylvania)
- "Cure You or Kill You: 19th-Century Medical Science and Quackery" (Laurel Hill Cemetery, Philadelphia, Pennsylvania)
- "Mischief, Murder, and Mayhem" (Mount Hope Cemetery, Rochester, New York; law breakers and enforcers)
- "Murder, Mayhem and Disasters" (Green-Wood Cemetery, Brooklyn, New York)
- "Lost at Sea" (Evergreen Cemetery, Portland, Maine; the 1898 SS *Portland* disaster)
- "Colt Monument Tour" (Cedar Hill Cemetery, Hartford, Connecticut)
- "In Death as in Life—Institutional Plots" (Mount Hope Cemetery, Rochester, New York)

Other Cemetery Education

In addition to walking tours, there are other types of educational activities occurring in cemeteries. One important example, which benefits not only the students but also the cemetery, is a stone preservation class. Congressional Cemetery in Washington, DC, held an "Operation Conservation" workshop in 2014 in which preservation organizations offered training and techniques on cemetery preservation. Elmwood Cemetery in Memphis, Tennessee, holds Elmwood University "Stone College," where participants learn the basics of cleaning and repairing monuments. After completion of the class, the volunteers assist in the cemetery by cleaning and resetting monuments. In addition to preservation training and workshops, cemeteries can teach about the granite industry in America, the changing customs of death and dying, and the modern burial process. Spring Grove Cemetery, in Cincinnati, Ohio, offers horticulture education classes. Other cemeteries offer offsite lectures or partner with local organizations to present educational lectures. Even when a walking tour isn't feasible, the cemetery can still be a place of education and training.

Cemetery Tours and Activities for Children

Cemeteries make great classrooms. Lessons and activities in history, art, math, science, and language are just a few of the subject areas in which cemetery activities can be developed. Using a cemetery to teach can help children to overcome their fears of burial grounds while also increasing

Figure 2.3.   Students in Laurel Hill Cemetery.
Source: Emma Stern.

their respect for the site. Many of the content-gathering suggestions previously mentioned can be adapted to fit a classroom group. In addition, the National Park Service's "Teaching with Historic Places" program (http://www.nps.gov/nr/twhp/) provides resources and ideas for developing lessons using sites on the National Register of Historic Places. Below are just a few examples of activities suited to the cemetery classroom.

Art

- Ask students to sketch a gravestone, adorn it with a symbol, and then give their opinion of what the symbol represents.
- Ask students to design their own headstone.

Geography

- Use a cemetery map and compass to find cemetery landmarks.

History

- Have students record every place of birth noted within a group of stones (or the entire cemetery).
- Have students conduct research on someone buried in the cemetery.

Language and Creative Writing

- Ask students to transcribe headstones and epitaphs and identify words they are unfamiliar with.
- Have students create a fictional epitaph for someone buried in the cemetery.

Math

- Have students record the year of birth and year of death from a section of headstones. Break down the age by male or female. Use those years to calculate the age of different individuals upon their death and the average age of the deceased from this group.
- Find the oldest burial and the newest burial. Subtract the newest from the oldest to try to determine the age of the cemetery.

Science

- Have students gather different leaves from across the cemetery and then identify the type of tree the leaves came from.
- Teach students to measure the circumference of a tree.
- Create descriptions of the birds you see during your visit to the cemetery.

Self-Guided Tours

When managers of antebellum rural cemeteries saw the huge numbers of visitors and tourists journeying to the grounds, they put together guide-books on the popular monuments in the cemetery. As cemeteries once again return as places of cultural tourism, guidebooks and self-guided tours educate people on the history of the cemetery. Even if there is not a formal tour scheduled, a self-guided tour allows visitors to explore the cemetery on their own time and with their own agenda. The most cost-effective way to produce a self-guided tour is with a paper map. Technology has enabled cemeteries to develop cell phone and digital app–based tours as well (see example on p. 57).

If developing a self-guided tour, include some of the same stops as you do on your formal introductory tour, but be aware of the difficulty most visitors will have navigating your grounds. Unless there are signs marking tour stops, or unless your app tour provides latitudinal and longitudinal locations, visitors will need clear directions to locate a grave. Including precise directions and a photograph of the monument are two keys to helping someone unfamiliar with the cemetery find the grave they are looking for.

Case Study 2.1: Teaching the Story of Our Past

I began working at Elmwood Cemetery on Veteran's Day in 1998. Still in college and pursing a degree in English, I had no idea of working at a cemetery at any point in my life. All I knew was that I wanted to work in the nonprofit sector, preferably in PR, and I wanted to make an impact for a cause I could believe in.

And then I stumbled into a job at a cemetery.

On that first day of what would become a passion for me, the cemetery staff was holding an event to memorialize the veterans of all U.S. wars. As my new coworkers and I left the building and headed out into the cem-

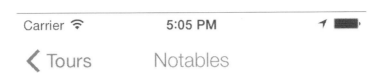

👤 Alexander Milne Calder

👤 Alexander Stirling Calder

👤 Alfred James Reach

Figure 2.4.   West Laurel Hill Cemetery digital app tour.
Source: webCemeteries.com.

Figure 2.5.   Kim McCollum in Elmwood Cemetery.
Photo by Willy Bearden.

etery for the event, I caught a lump rising in my throat. My grandfather had died just two months earlier; he was a veteran of World War II, and this was all entirely too overwhelming emotional for me. It was combined with the first-day jitters. At the event were children from the nearby elementary school, a veteran who fought in the Battle of the Bulge, a bugler who played "Taps," and a minister who led us in prayer. This was a foreign event for me. How could the people standing around *not* be moved to tears? I fought them back, but I lost, and I spent the rest of the day wishing my grandfather were still alive. I was unable to concentrate on my new gig. How was I supposed to be excited about *this*?

I went home that evening and told my mother that I wasn't going back. She listened, and suggested that I try it until the end of the week.

I hesitated before leaving for work the next morning, but I went in. I've been driving to the cemetery for almost eighteen years now, and I can't imagine working anywhere else or in any other industry.

I know you're reading this case study and wondering when I'm going to get to the part about youth education in a cemetery. I wrote my story to illustrate that successful programming begins with you. If you are new to this, you have to make peace with the concept of young children walking through the cemetery not to mourn but to learn. They'll be having fun, and this flies in the face of what we've been taught to believe cemeteries are supposed to be. You have to want to host groups of children, varying in age, educational level, and manners, and you have to treat them as your special guests. You have to believe in—and you have to make your bosses, staff, and volunteers feel—your love of and commitment to quality educational programming before you tell anyone not connected to your organization what your plans are. It starts with your mind-set.

But let's assume that your heart and your head are in sync and you're ready to put your program together. If you follow these steps, keep in mind that you'll be creating from scratch one tour that's going to be "remixed" (as my staff and I call it). You'll include several sites that will interest both adults and children, and ultimately your tour guides will be able to lead their tours and change their tone and timbre according to the group without having to learn multiple tour routes.

This is how to get started.

Read, Then Keep Reading

Read through your client files. If your cemetery is like mine, you're going to have file folders that contain various bits of information that are going to help you put a puzzle piece together. Take stock. What do you have? Even the slightest tidbit can be helpful to you if you keep an open mind. Do you know where your soldiers are buried? Make a list of the ones you know. You might make lists of poets, musicians, novelists, business people, masonic groups, suffragists, inventors . . . get creative with your thinking, and you'll be surprised what you know about your residents.

Side note: Keep not just your eyes but also your mind open. Does your cemetery have an abundance of trees? What about wildlife? Many cemeteries, especially older ones, are home to groundhogs, foxes, all types of birds, rabbits, chipmunks, and squirrels, to name a few. Other cemeteries are home to many different trees. At my cemetery, we have almost ninety different kinds of trees. This makes Elmwood a Level II Arboretum with the State of Tennessee's Urban Forestry department, and we even offer public and private tree tours. After you finish putting a history tour together, you can try something else.

Head's Up!

What are you located near? There's a major railroad bordering us, as well as a major African American college, a music museum, a very old and prominent church, an elementary school, a community center, a senior living facility—there are plenty of people and other longstanding institutions that might love to be treated to a sample tour, or they might like to learn how to be tour guides. What's just outside of your gate?

Who's There?

Walk the cemetery grounds with people who have never been to your cemetery. Ask your parents, your friends, teachers of science, history, English, even the funeral home directors you work with to go on a walk with you. Tell them that you're building a program and you wonder what it is they might like to learn about. As you walk, they'll ask questions about monuments that you've never considered. Be prepared for a lot of questions that you won't be able to answer. I used to (and sometimes still do) field questions that stump me. I've learned that it's okay to say that I don't know the answer, but that I'd be glad to look into it after the tour ends. I've found that visitors feel pretty good about stumping the tour guide—especially kids!

Of course, this is the point at which you're going to want to cast about specifically for a history teacher for help. Based on experience, I can tell you that tour groups younger than fifth-graders are not optimal tourists for cemetery tours. You can ask your librarian if they know of a fifth-to-sixth-grade history teacher who might be open to a request for help, but don't hesitate to ask a childhood education teaching student, or to visit your local Board of Education and ask them if they can recommend a teacher or teaching assistant to you. Why do you need this person?

A history teacher is going to offer great insight into what you're trying to accomplish. Ask them if they would create a set of lesson plans based on the tour you are about to create—preferably, ask if they'd donate these plans to the cause (don't forget to thank this person through social media and your newsletter!).

Ask, and Then Listen (And keep reading)

Familiarize yourself with the history of your city, county, and state, because this is going to set the context for your tour. Reading the Internet is going to be helpful to you, but there's no better way to really get to know your place like going to the library and talking with your librarians about what it is you want to do. You'll find that your city and university librarians are incredibly knowledgeable about local and state history, and they can point out vast resources that are never going to be available on the Internet. Librarians are also in-the-know when it comes to local history-based groups that you might end up working with to help grow your programs, perhaps as volunteer tour guides, so when I say be nice to the librarian, I mean be extra nice. You'll be rewarded with tons of help.

Now Get to Work

Organize your tour on paper and on the web.

1. Compose your tour. You're going to write no more than a page of information per each stop. Really, one page! No excuses. Take a photo of each stop and include it with your script. Plot each stop on a map. Save this document in a neat package that you can print out or email as needed.
2. With your completed document, you can recruit your staff and volunteers. Put out a note through social media for volunteers at a specific time and date. Pro tip: Don't make your training day a weekend day. Volunteers should be available on the same days that school groups will want tours. If a volunteer can't make it on a weekday, they probably won't be able to give tours to youth groups.

If your volunteers are anything like mine, they will be overwhelmed with emotions and information at first (so was I, remember?). We always tell our guides that they'll be ready to lead a group after they walk the cemetery tour three times. Find creative ways for your group to self-train. Have a good way of tracking the amount of time each volunteer donates to you. You'll want to have an appreciation event later on.

3. Have your administrative duties mapped out and assigned. Someone's going to have to take the tour reservations from teachers, contact and schedule volunteers, keep the website updated, and take on all sorts of administrative duties.

Now, Let Everyone Know

Somewhere on your website you need to upload those lesson plans and provide your tour information. This will include who gives the tours, what you can expect during your visit, when the cemetery will host school groups, where the cemetery is located, how many students you can accommodate, driving directions and where parking is located, and other basic information (you'll be surprised how many times you find yourself predicting the weather!). At my cemetery, we have a picnic area that can seat about forty, two restrooms, and a water fountain; teachers need to know this. How much will your tour cost per child, are teachers admitted free, and do chaperones or parents have to pay? Have these answers on the front end and, for the first few tours, stick steadfastly to the plan; you'll know how and when to bend your own rules later on, but in the beginning is not the time.

Call the Board of Education to request a meeting with a school liaison. Someone at an official level might need to approve the tour before you publicize. This will be the place where you find your teacher and principal email list, if they're willing to share it.

Write up a press release and contact local teachers. You'll only get a few hits at first, but that's optimal. It will give you a chance to work out the kinks.

Schedule your first tours with a ratio of one tour guide to twenty-five students. You're on your way to being able to boast a great community resource where once there was none. Good work!

As I've written this tutorial-of-sorts, I've been reflecting on the experiences I've had throughout my tenure at Elmwood. Tours have gone wrong. One time, a student who was in a tour group of mine slid into a pile of ginkgo berries and was covered in foul-smelling juice from head to toe. I've flubbed story deliveries and confused myself pretty thoroughly. I've had groups where no one listened and the teacher was totally checked out. It's pretty funny to think about in retrospect.

There have been so many more truly wonderful tour groups come through, too, and it's rewarding to talk to a group and know that they're listening and totally fascinated with what I'm saying. It's my passion for my work that's showing through, they tell me. There really is no greater compliment.

Good luck, and let me know how it turns out.

Kimberly McCollum is the executive director of Elmwood Cemetery in Memphis, Tennessee. Elmwood Cemetery is a historic cemetery with available lots that provides a beautiful final resting place to families as it shares its history, art, and nature with the community. Learn more about Elmwood at elmwoodcemetery.org, or contact Kim at kmccollum@elmwoodcemetery.org.

Case Study 2.2: Oakwood Cemetery's Science Lab

"Your cemetery hosts an NC Science Festival Event? Really?" is often a question that we're asked. The answer is, "Of course we do." Why? I ask you why not? But when the director of the state science festival proudly boasts that our partnership is the most unique one he has, we definitely know we are on to something good!

But in all seriousness, the answer to "Why science?" truly is "Why not?" A cemetery is many things to many people, but one thing we can all agree on is that a cemetery is an educational place. The types of education, however, are only limited by our imagination. History is the obvious topic of choice for many cemeteries, but to continue to show a cemetery's changing role in our community, it's important to think outside the box (no pun intended) in regard to other subjects that can be taught and learned on a cemetery's grounds.

Oakwood Cemetery elected to participate in the NC Science Festival for the first time in 2014 for two reasons. First, participating in events such as the NC Science Festival allowed us to continue our campaign of being good stewards of our land and for our community. We have the stories and the space to use our land in a community friendly way. And second, we want to expand our community's view of what a cemetery is. After all, we know we are a cemetery full of life, but we want our community to value our role as a good neighbor and to turn to us for unique opportunities for kids of all ages! What better way to challenge the status quo of a cemetery's role than to invite folks in and ask them to participate in a nontraditional cemetery activity!

We brainstormed first, "What kind of science could we offer?" We didn't want to be outlandish or too edgy. For 145 years we, for the most part, strictly played the "expected" role of a cemetery. We wanted to change the way we were viewed, but of course we needed to be respectful of the families that have chosen and continue to choose Oakwood as the final resting place for their loved ones. But we also wanted to show basic ways that we could demonstrate science on our grounds that directly related to what we have here. Any location can talk about science, but what makes up science at a cemetery? That's what we tried to achieve.

Also, we didn't want to entirely dismiss the idea of incorporating our history into the activities. After all, what is a cemetery without the stories of all who rest there? So for the first year of the NC Science Festival we created Cemetery Sleuths, a multitrack adventure that allowed visitors to assist Superintendent Sam in the solving of an old "mystery" while incorporating science and math at each activity. At the last stop of each track (which could only be reached by solving all of the previous activities correctly), participants received biographies of all of the graves they visited along the way. (Please note: We did use creative license in creating the mystery to make the story flow.)

So what type of science and math did we rely on? How did we come up with it? Well, we simply looked around our grounds! The two most prevalent things you see in our cemetery are headstones and trees. Therefore, we created activities that reflected both of those elements. We included using a compass and a guide to different types of trees to locate a specific tree, and then led participants to find the circumference of that particular tree. Each group was armed with a kit of supplies they would use throughout their journey; of course, string and a compass were included in each kit. We also created old receipts using historical funeral homes and estimating what prices were for headstones over one hundred years ago. Using a mathematical formula that we provided, we asked visitors to figure out the volume of a specific headstone. While that was difficult, we did provide hints to make it a little easier! (Calculators were also included in that kit.)

Using hydrochloric acid (on sample stones, not monuments), we asked visitors to determine which sample was marble and which sample was granite. (One will fizz when acid is squirted on a segment that has been scratched up—bet you didn't know that?!)

What did we put the kit supplies in? We couldn't expect, nor did we want, groups to go through the cemetery juggling hydrochloric acid, compasses, and yarn. So we went to our local funeral home and asked for a donation of the canvas bags that they transport urns in for funerals, or just after a cremation. It was perfect. And free. Don't be afraid to ask for donations. In this case, the company's name was on the bags, so it was free advertising for the funeral home, too. How could they say no?

Each kit also had a "passport" that allowed them to write down the answers to the questions from each station. That way it was quick and easy to submit at the end of the entire activity so we could "check" their answers. The passport was made in-house and was simple and inexpensive. We allowed participants to go through the stations in groups of at most ten so everyone would have a chance to go through the activities.

Soon we realized that science was truly everywhere on our grounds! Look to the right—see lichen on a headstone? That's a type of mold. So we researched and discovered a recipe for making your own lichen, and that became a take-home station. (See recipe and activity below.) We had a historic tree that had fallen a month earlier. We saved the stump and had the visitors count the rings to guess how old it was and had a binder full of photos of this historic tree being removed carefully from our grounds. These additional activities supplemented the Cemetery Sleuth main program. This helped us when there were lines waiting to check in as well as when groups were finished with Cemetery Sleuths but didn't yet want to leave. And the make-your-own-lichen station was a great takeaway for kids (and adults!).

And then we advertised. And I don't mean we paid money for advertisements, we used free options in our community. We advertised through the NC Science Festival website, of course, but also through our local media channels and their calendar of events. A standard press release stating that "Your Cemetery Hosts Science Festival Activities" released to your local media outlets is sure to turn heads and garner some media coverage. We also let local homeschooling organizations and the Boy Scouts and Girl Scouts know that we had a great educational and fun activity. It turns out that having a cemetery host science festival activities *is* pretty unique. We were named as one of the activities "not to miss" by local media outlets. That definitely helped to drum up some visitors!

To make sure we had enough volunteers to staff the three days of science activities (because we have a very small staff), we partnered with a local volunteer recruitment organization to recruit folks to cover shifts throughout the weekend. Again, the uniqueness of the opportunity assisted us in finding volunteers. Who doesn't want to see what their local cemetery is offering (besides funerals and grave space)?

Was it a success? Well, if you take out the unseasonably cold and rainy weather in North Carolina in April, yes, it was definitely a success! Over 150 people came through our grounds the first year we offered this program. And not just kids but adults who wanted to go through the stations and solve the mystery as well had a chance to enjoy the cemetery and the science that we offered. Our evaluations were overwhelmingly positive, and folks have come back with additional groups to participate on their own time. So it proved to not be only offered one time. But now, because we have the kits already made and ready to go, we can offer this as an educational opportunity to groups who want to learn about the cemetery. This type of program adds more depth to our current offerings of history activities, and it allows teachers to cover different or additional curriculum standards if they choose to come to the cemetery for activities. But that doesn't mean we had salespeople lurking behind trees, jumping out to answer questions! Staff was on hand, of course, but it was intentionally only an educational activity. We would lose all credibility if we tried to sell while educating the children.

You may be asking yourself, "What's the benefit if we put something like this together at our cemetery?" To be honest, we wondered that too. Is it worth our time to cater to children and their parents? To develop all of these activities that may only be used a few times a year? But it truly is a win-win. As stated earlier, we have the land and we have the educational opportunities, so why not do this? Bringing community members into your cemetery, regardless of age, helps to create generations of folks that will appreciate—and perhaps someday assist in preserving—your cemetery. Hosting a science festival event is just another way to make your cemetery more accessible to the community. And in today's world, it's a key component to a cemetery's life.

Sometimes, when I say that Oakwood Cemetery wants to be a good steward of its land, heads turn. To many folks, a cemetery company doesn't play that role, because aren't we putting concrete in the ground? Aren't people embalmed with chemicals? Yes, traditionally that is what we are, but we are so much more. In this day of urban redevelopment and tremendous growth in our communities, a cemetery is indeed a special place. If it weren't for sprawling garden cemeteries like ours, what would be here instead? When I see families walking through with strollers, kids learning to ride their bicycles on our roads, and joggers enjoying the 3.2

Figure 2.6.   Oakwood Cemetery Science Festival.
Photo courtesy of Kathryn King.

miles of roadways, I just smile. Because if this cemetery wasn't here, this land would have been turned into high rises or big-box stores. This land instead was set aside by city leaders over a century ago for the most sacred purpose—a resting place for the community's dead—and with that purpose came a design that was to serve the entire community.

PS: We did participate in the 2015 NC Science Festival, too! In 2015 we offered The Birds & The Bees of Oakwood Cemetery. For this activity we relied on the fact that we have three beehives on the North Carolina Blue Bird Trail. We set up stations in the open acreage of our cemetery (as opposed to using the historic sections the prior year) and had participants earn "honey" points at each station to achieve graduation at Oakwood Academy. Stations included making their own bee's wax candle, identifying the parts of a bee, and trying on a bee suit as well as observing Eastern Blue Birds in their habitat, scavenging for food the way a blue bird does, and so on. Some two hundred folks enjoyed the 2015 Science Festival at Oakwood Cemetery.

Superintendent Sam's Lichen Slurry Booth

"Traditional" Formula
Simply paint milk onto the surface that you want the lichen to grow on.

"Magnificent Lichen Growth Formula" (from lichenlovers.org)

¼ cup of milk
½ tsp flour
¼ tsp gelatin
½ tbs green algae powder
⅙ tbs water-soluble fertilizer

Robin Simonton is the executive director at Oakwood Cemetery.

Notes

1. Strangstad, *A Graveyard Preservation Primer*, 33–34.
2. Jewish Genealogical Society, http://www.jgsny.org/ny-burial-society-database.
3. Meyer, *Cemeteries & Gravemarkers*, 2.
4. Bronner, *American Material Culture and Folklife*, 14.
5. Foster and Hummel, "The Adkins-Woodson Cemetery," 94–95.
6. Fenza, "Communities of the Dead," 139.
7. Fenza, "Communities of the Dead," 147.
8. Tiffany Glass and Decorating Company, "Out-of-Door Memorials."
9. Edgette, "The Epitaph and Personality Revelation," 89.
10. McDowell and Meyer, *The Revival Styles in American Memorial Art*, 15.
11. Yalom, *The American Resting Place*, 28.

12. McDowell and Meyer, *The Revival Styles in American Memorial Art*, 4.

13. Potter and Boland, "Guidelines for Evaluating and Registering Cemeteries and Burial Places," 21.

14. McGahee and Edmonds, *South Carolina's Historic Cemeteries*, 24.

15. Levy, Lloyd, and Schreiber, *Great Tours!* 108.

Recreation
Using Cemeteries as Parks

Cemeteries and parks have always had a complex relationship. At the start of the 1830s when the first rural cemeteries were founded, municipal parks were not yet a part of the American experience. When Mount Auburn, Laurel Hill, and Green-Wood opened, thousands of visitors flocked to these cemeteries, whether to stroll, take a carriage ride, or to admire the trees, monuments, and sculptures. Landscape designer Andrew Jackson Downing pointed to the success of these early cemeteries in his quest for the establishment of municipal parks. At the same time, he lamented the fact that cemeteries were being used more for leisure than for reflection, writing, "The only draw back to these beautiful and highly kept cemeteries, to my taste, is the gala-day air of *recreation* they present. People seem to go there to enjoy themselves, and not to indulge in any serious recollections or regrets."[1]

Downing wasn't the only American concerned with the use of cemeteries for recreational purposes. Managers of these first-generation rural cemeteries all had to come to terms with the overwhelming popularity of the sites, and many instituted rules and restrictions to keep behavior under control. Laurel Hill Cemetery trustees were concerned about "casual" visitation as early as 1844 (less than a decade after opening). Minutes from a meeting of the managers in January 1844 note the topic as being "one of great interest to those concerned," as lot holders were increasingly troubled by the admittance of the general public and the privilege of admittance "being liable to abuse from others than lotholders taking advantage of the ignorance or credulity of the Gatekeeper."[2] By the end of 1847 the managers had decided to prohibit the general public from entering during the weekends, instead restricting admittance to lot owners who were issued a ticket.

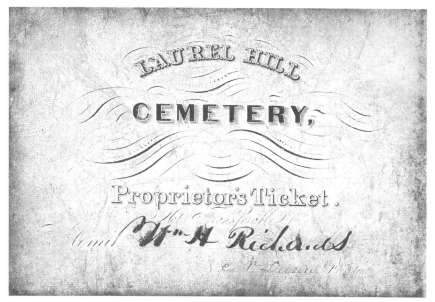

Figure 3.1.   Laurel Hill Cemetery lot holder's ticket, ca. 1847.
Source: Laurel Hill Cemetery.

The implementation of a ticket system was advertised in the local newspaper, and even guidebooks noted the use of a ticket system to keep out "improper persons."[3]

As major cities began to establish public parks, however (construction would begin on New York's Central Park in 1857), the use of cemeteries for purposes of recreation began to wane. Tourists and the public could turn to public gardens or parks to stroll or take a carriage ride. The establishment of museums and art galleries further eroded the cemetery's recreational patronage as Americans found other places to spend their free time. Cemeteries became one-dimensional places for disposal; by the end of the nineteenth century, they were no longer vital elements of a community's recreational experience.

Slowly, in recent decades, this trend has begun to reverse itself, as visitors rediscover cemeteries as sites for recreational and leisure activities. For contemporary cemeteries, bringing people through the gates begins the process of getting them invested in the site's welfare. Undoubtedly, many people are already using their local cemetery for recreational purposes—possibly to walk their dog, ride a bike, or just walk and explore—but the decision to market recreational activities is not always a clear-cut one. Cemeteries across the nation have vastly different rules when it comes to dog walking, jogging, biking, and other physical activities. While some restrict these activities, others specifically market to pet owners and runners. Some (like Historic Oakland Cemetery in Atlanta, Georgia) even refer to themselves as public parks and are owned, in part, by the city. Other cemeteries maintain strict prohibitions on who comes through their gates and what activities they engage in while there, emphasizing their status as private organizations. Still others are corporate entities beholden only to shareholders. With open space shrinking in communities across the nation, recreational and leisure activities present cemeteries—regardless of their ownership model—with another way to engage members of the public and to begin the process of getting them invested in the preservation of the burial ground.

This chapter will look at various opportunities for recreational and leisure activities and suggest ways to develop such programming, focusing on physical activities, arts programming, and hobbies or leisure activities.

What Can You Do In a Park?

When thinking about recreational activities in a cemetery, first ask the question, "What can you do in a park?" and then figure out how and if those activities can be translated to a cemetery. There are some event programmers using cemeteries who try to "take the cemetery out of it," an impossible task, for many. They attempt to create programming that will allow participants to experience the space as a park, not as a repository for the dead. To consider the cemetery a park means, in part, to think of it more in terms of leisure and recreation than in terms of history and material culture. In some ways, a cemetery is well suited for physical activities such as walking, bike riding, and dog walking, as the paved roads, isolated from heavy traffic, provide a safe environment. In other ways, recreational activities might seem offensive to mourners grieving the loss of a loved one. Yet while some perceive recreational use as disrespectful to the dead, others find it a means of keeping ancestors in the forefront of their minds. Because there are no firm guidelines on appropriate behavior in a cemetery, each institution must reckon individually with the question of recreational use, with sensitivity to various constituencies and awareness of potential liability issues. It is important to address these concerns in advance in order to protect the cemetery. The items discussed in this chapter cannot be recreated everywhere, but they can act as inspiration and serve as examples of the kinds of recreational activities cemeteries can host.

Evaluating Cemetery Space with an Eye for Recreation

Before undertaking any recreation/leisure event planning for a cemetery, it is important to assess the site with an eye both to aesthetics and practical considerations. It is not enough to merely have a good idea; the physical components of the cemetery must render the idea feasible. Different activities, ranging from yoga to concerts to theatrical performances, demand different settings. Once the practical questions are addressed, it is time to consider which spaces in the cemetery are most visually interesting. Whether a picturesque scenic overlook, a water feature, or a particularly compelling sculpture, the visual backdrop for recreational activities can greatly impact their success.

The following questions are helpful guides for determining how the cemetery space can be used. If the cemetery has a map, marking these areas will help you to visualize the use of space.

1. What are the open areas (if any) with no graves? Particularly for "active" cemeteries (those continuing to do burials), this is an essential question to ask.
2. Which areas have fewer or no burials, and which see regular use?
3. What special aspects of the landscape can lend itself to your event? Are there natural sloping areas that could act as a stage? Do hills, trees, or winding paths provide needed seclusion?
4. What roads or paths will visitors use to access the space?
5. Are the chosen areas accessible by car or only by foot? If accessible by car, are there ample parking and adequate signage?
6. How far is the walk from public transportation? What landmarks can be used to help direct visitors to the event?
7. Where are the restrooms?
8. How will traffic flow, both into the event and following its conclusion? Even with the most scenic location, a spot requiring too much walking (both from restrooms and parking) quickly becomes unfeasible.
9. Where is there electricity within the cemetery? Lights?
10. Where is there water?
11. Are there options for moving the event indoors in case of rain? In addition to considering indoor space in case of inclement weather, it helps to consider ways in which the event might be adapted should weather conditions worsen. One of the challenges in creating cemetery programming is adjusting to and preparing for the weather.

Physical Recreational Activities

The following is a partial list of recreational activities currently occurring in cemeteries across the nation:

1. walking and hiking trails
2. competitive races and fun runs
3. dog walks
4. yoga
5. Segway tours
6. bike riding
7. snowshoeing and cross-country skiing

Walking Trails

Countless cemeteries are already regularly being used as walking trails. Paved trails and roadways, limited traffic traveling at low speeds, and interesting landscapes make cemeteries ideal places for daily exercise. Merely opening cemetery gates will attract recreation seekers such as walkers and bike riders, but there are many more ways to attract the public. One option is to become listed as a National Recreation Trail. The National Trails System Act of 1968 authorized the creation of a national network composed of National Recreation Trails, National Scenic Trails, and National Historic Trails to help promote outdoor recreation and good stewardship of the land.[4] Among the benefits of receiving this designation are promotional opportunities as well as training and resource opportunities. People looking for a local trail can find one by a searchable database. Designation as a National Recreation Trail also lets the public know the cemetery is not strictly for burying the dead but also for promoting health and wellness for the living.

If your cemetery is already open for recreational walking, or looking to invite limited recreation, look for websites where it can be listed. Many communities have local or regional sites listing trails. Evergreen Cemetery in Portland, Maine, for example, is a historic cemetery open to several different types of recreation. Evergreen's listings on the websites healthy-mainewalks.com, mainetrailfinder.com, and the Portland Trails website will attract new visitors to the cemetery. You might also consider offering a walking club. Depending upon the cemetery's location, it might be easily accessible to workers during their lunch hours. Crown Hill Funeral Home and Cemetery in Indianapolis takes its walking club a step further by recording mileage and offering prizes for miles walked.

Another way to promote recreational activities in a cemetery is to connect with a larger existing walking trail. Many communities have walking trails, whether it's a "rails to trails" path along a former railroad line, a scenic walk along a river, or a historic walking trail of the community. Connecting the cemetery, whether it be a stop on the trail or opening a new access point, makes more miles of walking space available for trail users, while exposing this audience to the cemetery's art, architecture, and arboretum. Even those who have never been to a cemetery for a nonfuneral reason might venture inside the gates if given the opportunity. Once inside, they are better able to appreciate the space as a type of museum or outdoor sculpture garden.

Becoming part of a state or local outdoor program is a good way to attract audiences who might be unaware of the cemetery's status as a place of recreation. Cedar Hill Cemetery in Hartford, Connecticut, has promoted itself as a walking trail by becoming part of Connecticut Trail Days Weekend. This annual event (held as part of the National Trails Day celebration) occurs the first weekend of June and features more than two hundred events across the state of Connecticut. Cedar Hill hosts a "Tree Buffs" tour and benefits from the publicity that makes the public—including those unable to participate on that particular day—aware of the site as a walking trail.

West Laurel Hill Cemetery, located just outside of Philadelphia, was able to promote itself as a space for walking by partnering with the Cynwyd Heritage Trail, a route created through an unused and overgrown former Schuylkill Division Pennsylvania Railroad line. When the railroad was in use, West Laurel Hill had an entrance to admit funeral processions arriving by train from Philadelphia. When the heritage trail was established, West Laurel Hill became a trail partner, donating funds, meeting space, and stone mile markers; volunteering for workdays and committees; and helping to publicize the trail and trail-related events. With the opening of the long-abandoned entrance to the cemetery from the railroad, trail visitors can now easily access the cemetery. In addition, historical signage, picnic tables, benches, and dog waste containers close to the cemetery entrance make trailgoers aware they are welcome on the cemetery grounds. West Laurel Hill has also partnered with the heritage trail on health-related programming, such as a 5K run and wellness talks on topics such as skin care and hydration. In 2015, a weekly farmers' market held at the trail entrance to the cemetery brought even more new visitors onto the cemetery grounds.

Figure 3.2.   Entrance to the Cynwyd Heritage Trail from West Laurel Hill.
Photo by author.

Figure 3.3.   Ocmulgee Heritage Trail, Riverside Cemetery, Macon, Georgia.
Photo by author.

Another cemetery connected with a walking trail is Riverside Cemetery in Macon, Georgia. The Ocmulgee Heritage Trail runs along Riverside Cemetery, and a tributary runs through the cemetery. Riverside built a boardwalk with an observation deck, which links in with the trail. In addition to the recreation component, Riverside Cemetery Conservancy plans to develop educational public programming and activities centered on nature. Historic Oakland Cemetery in Atlanta is connected with a different type of trail, the *Gone with the Wind* Trail. As the final resting place for Margaret Mitchell, author of the best-selling book, Oakland welcomes visitors who come to the cemetery as part of the pilgrimage to *Gone with the Wind* sites. Woodland Cemetery and Arboretum in Dayton, Ohio, the burial place of Wilbur and Orville Wright, is featured as part of Dayton's Aviation Trail. Becoming linked with an existing walking trail will draw in new visitors who may never have visited a cemetery for recreation.

Philadelphia's Laurel Hill Cemetery is also attempting to draw a new group of recreation-minded visitors to the cemetery by opening a long-closed entrance. Every day, thousands of commuters use Kelly Drive, which borders the site's western edge, on their way to and from Center City, Philadelphia. From the road, Laurel Hill can look interesting—but foreboding. The bluffs protect the cemetery from traffic while the statues and mausoleums visible from the roadway inspire attention and curiosity. Laurel Hill is attempting to capture a percentage of that daily traffic by opening a new entrance to the cemetery from Kelly Drive. The vision is to draw in this new audience by making access to the cemetery easier. Boosting visitation will draw more people to programs, which in turn will increase membership. Eventually the cemetery plans to open an orientation center near the Kelly Drive entrance and offer amenities such as bike racks, benches, and concessions in the hope of helping the public to see the cemetery as a safe and green space available for public use.

Not every cemetery will be interested in recreational activities, but the interest and openness will only grow as other open spaces in surrounding communities become lost to development.

Competitive Races and Fun Runs

The past decade has seen a nationwide surge in cemetery runs. Cemeteries can be ideal places for running, and many are capitalizing on this by creating both competitive races and fun runs. Cemetery runs frequently have several common features.

1. A fun name. Laurel Hill Cemetery has a "Rest in Peace 5K." Historic Oakland does the "Run Like Hell Pushing Up Daisies 5K." Rosehill Cemetery holds a "Crypt 5K Run and Walk." In Delaware's Wilmington and Brandywine Cemetery, there is the "Eternal Rest 5K Run/Walk." "The Screaming Pumpkin 5K" takes place in Springdale Cemetery, in Peoria, Illinois. In Dayton's Woodland Cemetery the "Free Your Sole 5K" race crosses the cemetery grounds. Congressional Cemetery, located in Washington, D.C., even holds a "Day of the Dog 5K," where competitors run alongside their dogs. These names let participants know that this is no ordinary race and certainly not a typical race location.
2. Frequently Halloween and costume related. While a few of these races attract serious runners (Oakland's race is a Peachtree Road Race qualifier and Historic Spring Grove Cemetery has a USATF-certified 5K course), these are usually fun runs, where costumes are encouraged. The Screaming Pumpkin 5K even takes place at night under the light of the moon.
3. These races are fund-raisers. While most often benefiting the cemetery itself, proceeds from these races may, in some cases, be donated to other charitable organizations.
4. It's all about the after party. From beer and food to music, most cemetery runs hold a party following the race. Food trucks are popular choices for this kind of event as they are self-contained and usually offer interesting food choices.

Cemeteries looking to draw in an audience seeking recreational activities and fitness, as well as running or health clubs looking for a new and different way to attract runners, should consider a cemetery as a memorable location for a run. Developing a run, however, demands a number of important considerations.

- Will the race be a competitive, timed race or a fun run? Will more than one race take place that day? Will there be an alternative for those wishing to walk the route?
- Will the race have a theme? Will that theme be cemetery or death related?
- Will there be an entry fee? What will that fee cover? Will you allow preregistration? Will you allow teams or have a special award for team winners?

- What partners can be enlisted to help promote, organize, and sponsor an event? What should be asked and expected of partners? Look to partner with a local running club or gym, as they will have access to the audiences most inclined to sign up for a run.
- What kinds of sponsors can you approach for food, entertainment, monetary contributions, or prizes?
- What possible liability issues could the cemetery face? Will participants sign waivers? Do partners and vendors have sufficient insurance? How will you have first aid available, and who will administer it?
- Will you provide water and water stations for participants?
- What after-party vendors (food, music, alcohol) should be included?
- Will there be prizes?
- Where can the event be publicized?

Woof, Wag 'n' Walk: Dogs and Cemeteries

In using a cemetery for recreation for dogs and their human companions, there's a wide spectrum in terms of accepted activities. Some cemeteries prohibit dogs completely. Others allow dogs but with restrictions: they may require dogs to be on leashes, walk only in certain areas of the cemetery, or visit only during certain hours. Others may provide water bowls and dog waste containers but do not specifically market events and services to dog owners and their canines. Spring Grove Cemetery and Arboretum in Cincinnati opens its gates to dogs one day a year when holding a "Dog Day of Summer" event. Some cemeteries take a more active approach to attracting dogs and their owners. West Laurel Hill Cemetery has a "Woof, Wag 'n' Walk" event featuring a variety of dog vendors, nonprofit animal welfare organizations and shelters, and a walking tour of the cemetery where the guide makes dog-related stops. Each year donations are collected for a local dog-related nonprofit organization. The event not only attracts dog lovers but also provides information on the cemetery through the walking tour.

Whitehaven Memorial Park in Pittsford, New York, developed pet-friendly hiking trails. The Woodlands, a cemetery in Philadelphia, has a Dog of the Month feature in its cemetery newsletter. Hollywood Cemetery in Richmond, Virginia, offers "History Hounds" tours, and Elmwood Cemetery in Memphis offers "Pawing through History," dog-friendly history walking tours. All of these activities make it clear to the public that dogs are welcome on cemetery grounds.

The cemetery that takes dogs to another level, however, is Congressional Cemetery in Washington, D.C. Congressional allows dogs to be walked off leash in the cemetery as part of a membership in the "K9 Corps." This

Figure 3.4.   Woof, Wag 'n' Walk at West Laurel Hill Cemetery.
Photo by author.

approach has proven to be a major source of income (bringing in about
20 percent of the annual operating budget),[5] with demand so high that
there is always a long waiting list. The program also brings in volunteers.
In addition to dues, members have to volunteer eight hours per year. With
around six hundred K9 Corps members in 2014, that's nearly five thousand

volunteer hours. In fact, the dog program at Congressional has turned into a major way to preserve a cemetery placed on the National Trust for Historic Preservation's 1997 list of America's 11 Most Endangered Places.

The history of the corps goes back to the mid-1990s, when a group of regular Congressional dog walkers began to organize as the K9 Corps. The K9 Corps became an official organization of the Association for the Preservation of Historic Congressional Cemetery in 2007. It has its own board of directors and committees, maintains rules, and sets the maximum number of dogs. In addition to this unique program, Congressional features several dog-related events. They have "Yappy Hours," which usually occur once a month. These casual events allow K9 Corps dogs and members to socialize. They also have a Day of the Dog Festival, which features local

Figure 3.5.   Day of the Dog at Congressional Cemetery.
Photo by author.

dog vendors, humane shelters and rescue organizations, live music, food trucks, activities such as bobbing for hot dogs, agility and obstacle courses, contests and training demonstrations, a 5K run for dogs and their owners, and many dogs!

Allowing dogs and creating dog-related events in a cemetery creates a unique set of issues to address both with the public and in executing an event or tour.

- Be prepared for complaints, and be able to defend your decision to allow dogs in the cemetery. As much as dog lovers might have a difficult time comprehending this fact, not everyone loves dogs, and some people are extremely frightened of them. Be prepared to justify their presence in the cemetery and treat any complaint with consideration and respect.
- Have dog waste bags and containers available at entrances to the cemetery. Having waste receptacles stationed in the cemetery encourages members of the public to dispose of their dog's waste, and also shows that dogs are welcome in the cemetery.
- Gradually introduce the concept of dogs in the cemetery, and work up to holding official events.
- Consider partnering with local animal shelters or rescues. They will be able to promote your event and reach an audience of dog lovers. They might also be willing to bring dogs needing homes to your event. Puppies, especially, are always crowd-pleasers. Accept and solicit donations for these partner organizations among your event participants.

Leading a tour or dog walk in a cemetery presents its own set of challenges. Here are a few tips:

- Keep moving! Downtime leads to dog trouble. Even the best-behaved dogs can get restless when stopping for a long time while surrounded by other dogs. Avoid potential canine conflicts by making any stops brief.
- Have a way to create a shorter walk for smaller dogs by cutting the tour short for the small dogs or having two groups. Be aware that most small dogs do not have the stamina the larger dogs have.
- Have water stations or carry water along the way.
- Carry dog-waste bags and a trash bag along on the tour.

Cemeteries for Leisure Activities

In addition to physical recreational activities, cemeteries can be used for other leisure activities, including:

- as garden spaces
- birding
- photography

The formal events and programming created to support these types of activities can also be educational in nature.

Cemeteries as Garden Spaces

The first-generation rural or "garden" cemeteries were designed by horticulturists with the intention of creating a type of public garden. Mount Auburn was founded with guidance from the Massachusetts Horticultural Society. John Notman, Laurel Hill's architect, created a cemetery inspired by English garden design. The Woodlands was developed on the grounds of the estate of a late eighteenth-century plant collector and botanist William Hamilton. The connection between cemeteries and horticulture continues today, and creates other opportunities for utilization of a cemetery for alternative uses.

The primary way cemeteries maintain themselves as garden spaces is by caring for their arboreta. Particularly among the rural cemeteries, these areas can feature outstanding examples of specimen trees and shrubs. Many rural cemeteries employ professional gardeners, horticulturalists, and arborists to care for the numerous trees and other plantings on their grounds. These sites often offer tours showcasing state champion trees or notable specimens. Cemeteries can use horticulture programming and classes to attract community members interested in learning about gardens and cultivating techniques showcased in their institution. Cemeteries can also act as the stage for a festival featuring a seasonal plant or celebration, such as Mountain View Cemetery's Pumpkin Festival, which features free activities, treats, and pumpkins for children. Several other cemeteries hold events featuring spring's bright flower, the daffodil.

In addition to trees, some cemeteries maintain special gardens. Spring Grove Cemetery and Arboretum in Cincinnati (the first cemetery to develop the landscape "lawn plan" featuring more open grassy areas) maintains an All-America Selections Display Garden. AAS is a nonprofit organization that determines the best performers in flowers and vegetables. In a display garden, the public can view these new cultivars. Spring Grove also offers educational walks such as "Woody Plant Identification," where the cemetery's horticulturalists point out some of the cemetery's most unique or interesting plants. Hollywood Cemetery, located in Richmond, Virginia, maintains approximately 130 rose bushes, some of which may be at least one hundred years old. In addition to a self-guided walking tour showing the location of notable roses, Hollywood holds an annual Rose Day, when volunteers organize to prune the bushes. Old City Cemetery, located in Lynchburg, Virginia, was established in 1806. Marketing itself as a public garden and "history park," the "gravegarden" includes an orchard, memorial shrub garden, roses, medicinal herb garden, and antique daffodil collection.[6] As showcases for unique or rare plants, these cemetery spaces can be marketed to people interested in horticulture and gardening.

Volunteer gardeners work in many cemeteries across the nation; however, specialized instruction can be essential in maintaining the health of some plants. Cemeteries wishing to restore historical plantings or gardens will also require specialized help to identify plants that would have been used at a certain point in the cemetery's history. Researching what was planted in the cemetery's past, along with an understanding of which cultivars might have been available during a certain period of time, can aid with development. Historical and current landscape plans can reveal changes occurring over time that have altered the look of the cemetery landscape, such as the addition or removal of paths, walls, fences, or flowerbeds.

If considering developing or building upon the garden aspects of a cemetery:

- Survey or identify trees and plantings, noting any unique, rare, or specimen trees or examples.
- If staff is limited, develop a group of volunteer gardeners or contact local garden clubs for assistance.
- Consult trained horticulturalists or other experts.
- Create an "in bloom" list of plants, trees, and flowers, indicating where and when they will be in bloom.
- Consider acting as a site to host a seasonal festival.

Birding

The concept of cemeteries as bird sanctuaries has existed nearly as long as the modern American cemetery, and the leisure activity of birdwatching (or birding) is even longer. As early as 1870, due to the growing attraction of Mount Auburn as a place for birdwatching, the Mount Auburn Trustees established a Committee on Birds to recommend plantings that would attract birds.[7] T. Gilbert Pearson, conservationist and a founder of what

Figure 3.6.   Red tail hawk on sculpture, Laurel Hill Cemetery.
Photo by Frank P. Rausch III.

would become the National Audubon Society, wrote in his 1917 text, *The Bird Study Book*, "Throughout this country there should be a concerted effort to convert the cemeteries, the homes of our friends who have gone away, into sanctuaries for the bird life of this land. And what isolated spots could be more welcome to the birds than these places that hold so many sad memories for human beings?"[8] In the early twentieth century, industry publications such as *Park and Cemetery and Landscape Gardening* published articles on the efforts to attract birds by cemeteries across the nation, and the benefits of creating a bird-friendly environment in a cemetery. Similar articles appeared in nature-related journals and magazines.

In the Philadelphia area in 1914, Laurel Hill and West Laurel Hill Cemeteries installed several hundred feeders and birdhouses with the hope of attracting birds. Management saw this not only as an effort to make the cemetery "more cheerful and attractive to the thousands of visitors" but also as a utilitarian effort to manage the "insect pests which would otherwise injure the beautiful flowers, trees and shrubbery in these sanctuaries."[9] And in 1916, a cemetery in Omaha, Nebraska, proclaimed itself as the largest cemetery bird sanctuary in America. The man responsible for this effort,

H. S. Mann, advocated for all cemeteries to become protected areas for birds, even approaching the Audubon Society to join his campaign.[10] These movements to provide safe havens for birds in cemeteries have continued into the twenty-first century, with both local organizations and national and international organizations such as Audubon International promoting conservation and the creation of bird-friendly habitats in cemeteries.

The reasons for advocating the use of cemeteries to attract birds are fairly obvious. Their relative quiet and seclusion, combined with the importance of vegetation and plantings, create a welcoming environment. Cemeteries like Mount Auburn have been and continue to be havens for birds, perhaps even more so now than in the nineteenth century due to the increased development and destruction of birds' natural habitats. Indeed, in cemeteries nationwide, opportunities to develop educational programs and activities related to these important cemetery visitors continue to engage cemetery programmers, community conservancies, and birding societies.

One of the first steps when developing bird-related programming is to consider how to create an environment to attract birds. While cemeteries are naturally advantageous environments due to their relative isolation and quiet, there are a number of ways to enhance the landscape to attract birds. These efforts will be most effective when partnering with an ornithologist, bird club, or other organization whose members are knowledgeable about local birds and their habitats.

- *Birdhouses.* The construction of birdhouses and the placement of these boxes is one effective way to attract birds. In some instances, local scout troops can be counted upon to build and help install boxes as part of a service project.
- *Food and water.* Another way to attract birds is to provide food sources—such as feeders or bushes with berries—as well as water sources.
- *Natural environments.* Allowing for natural vegetation and growth instead of finely manicuring the grounds creates bird-friendly places for nesting. Decisions about how the grass is mowed, how trees are pruned and managed, and what pesticides and herbicides can be safely used may all affect birds and whether they are attracted to and can thrive in a cemetery.

The activity of birdwatching or birding has been an important part of the American leisure experience for centuries, and it is one of the most popular and fastest growing hobbies in America. According to a report by the U.S. Fish and Wildlife Service, there were forty-seven million birders (age sixteen or older) in the United States in 2011.[11] With so many people having more than just a passing interest in birdlife, there is tremendous potential for increasing cemetery visitation by creating programming and events or even just setting up an environment to attract both birds and birders.

One place to start is with documenting the bird species present in the cemetery. This task usually requires expert assistance from an organization able not only to identify the birds seen but also to discover when they are likely to appear and how common they are.

Figure 3.7 is a partial listing of the species of birds documented at West Laurel Hill Cemetery and the adjoining Cynwyd Heritage Trail. Dr. Gregg Gorton, a member of the local Lower Merion Conservancy who documented birds at the cemetery for more than fifteen years, compiled the list. This spreadsheet not only captures the names of the roughly 140 bird species seen in the area, but it also indicates how common they were and when they were most likely to be seen. Making such a list available will let birders know what types of birds they can expect to see in the area. Cemeteries without an existing bird inventory can invite a local bird club to come and do a survey as a starting point to documenting the species residing there. And along with a bird checklist, some cemeteries, like Mount Auburn, also provide information on birdwatching etiquette and guidelines for self-guided birders. In addition to offering guided bird tours, other cemeteries are offering an up-close view of birds by bringing in speakers and bird handlers for events featuring owls or other birds of prey.

In some ways, a bird tour can be one of the most dynamic tours given in a cemetery. Different birds will be present at different times of the year, and they will be engaged in fascinatingly varied activities during different seasons—whether setting up territories after returning from migration, courting, building nests, brooding and then feeding young, teaching the fledglings essential hunting skills, engaging in other family behaviors, or gathering in flocks before the next migration. A bird walk can address where a cemetery's birds like to nest, the type of homes they build (or cavities they excavate and use), and where best to look for these homes. Tours should note the trees and shrubs that attract birds, whether for food or habitat. Never forget the soundscape: by tuning in to the aural ambiences of songs and calls, tour leaders can help familiarize the group with a critically important way of identifying the species in a cemetery. Finally, by looking at the way birds are represented on the markers and monuments, whether in the form of iconography or epitaphs, the tour can be tied back to the unique environment that is the cemetery.

In addition to bird-focused walking tours, a popular event that can be held in a cemetery is a bird count. A bird count may be a purely local event,

The following bird species have been documented at West Laurel Hill Cemetery and the adjoining Cynwyd Heritage Trail. Their seasonal prevalence is also listed. Please let us know if you spot a species not listed.

Species	Sp	Su	F	W
Common Loon ^	V		V	
Dbl-crest Cormorant ^	U	U	U	
Green-backed Heron ^	U	U	U	
Great Blue Heron ^	V		V	R
Tundra Swan ^	V		V	V
Canada Goose *	C	C	C	C
Snow Goose ^	R		R	R
Wood Duck	U	U	U	V
Canvasback ^	V		V	V
Northern Shoveler ^	V		V	V
Mallard *	C	C	C	C
Northern Pintail ^	V		V	V
Common Merganser	U	U	U	C
Black Vulture ^	U	U	U	C
Turkey Vulture ^	C	C	C	C
Osprey ^	R	R	R	
Bald Eagle ^	V		R	
Northern Harrier ^	R		R	
Sharp-shinned Hawk ^	U	U	U	U
Cooper's Hawk *	C	U	C	U
Northern Goshawk ^	R		R	R
Red-shouldered Hawk ^	U		U	
Broad-winged Hawk ^	U		U	
Red-tailed Hawk *	C	C	C	C
American Kestrel ^	U	U	U	U
Merlin ^			R	R
Peregrine Falcon ^	U	U	R	R
Wild Turkey			U	U
Killdeer ^	R	R	R	V
Spotted Sandpiper	R	R	R	
Ring-billed Gull ^	C	U	A	A
Laughing Gull ^	R	R	R	
Herring Gull ^	R	R		
Great Black-backed Gull ^	U	R		
Bonaparte's Gull				V
Greater Scaup				V
Bufflehead			R	
Ring-necked Duck				V
American Black Duck	U	U	U	
Hooded Merganser			R	R
Pied-billed Grebe			R	R

Species	Sp	Su	F	W
Rock Dove * ^	A	A	A	A
Mourning Dove *	C	C	C	C
Yellow-billed Cuckoo	U	U	U	
Eastern Screech-owl	U	U	U	U
Great Horned Owl *	U	U	U	R
Common Nighthawk ^	U	V	C	
Chimney Swift ^	A	A	A	
Ruby-thr't Hummingbird *	U	U	U	
Belted Kingfisher	U	U	U	R
Red-bellied Woodpecker *	C	C	C	C
Yel-bell'd Sapsucker	U		C	C
Downy Woodpecker *	C	C	C	C
Hairy Woodpecker *	C	C	C	R
Northern Flicker *	C	C	C	C
Eastern Wood-Pewee *	R	R	R	
Acadian Flycatcher *	R	R		
Willow Flycatcher	U	U		
Least Flycatcher	C	C	C	
Eastern Phoebe *	C	C	C	V
Great-cr'd Flycatcher *	U	U	R	
Eastern Kingbird *	C	C		
Tree Swallow *	C	C	C	
N Rough-winged Swallow *	R	R	R	
Bank Swallow ^	R	R	R	
Barn Swallow ^	C	C	C	
Blue Jay *	C	C	C	C
American Crow * ^	C	C	C	C
Fish Crow	U	U	U	R
Black-capped Chickadee	R	R	R	R
Carolina Chickadee *	C	C	C	C
Tufted Titmouse *	C	C	C	C
Red-br'd Nuthatch	R	R	R	R
White-br'd Nuthatch *	C	C	C	C
Brown Creeper	U	U	R	U
Carolina Wren *	C	C	C	C
House Wren *	C	C	C	V
Winter Wren	R	R	U	U
Golden-cr'd Kinglet	C	C	C	C
Ruby-cr'd Kinglet	C	C	C	R
Blue-gray Gnatcatcher *	U	U	U	
Veery	U	U		
Gray-cheeked Thrush	U	U		
Swainson's Thrush	U	U		
Saw-Whet Owl			V	V
American Woodcock			R	

Species	Sp	Su	F	W
Hermit Thrush	U		U	R
Wood Thrush *	C	A	U	
American Robin *	A	A	A	C
Gray Catbird *	C	C	C	V
Northern Mockingbird *	C	C	C	U
Brown Thrasher *	U	V	C	
Cedar Waxwing *	U	U	U	R
European Starling *	A	A	A	C
White-eyed Vireo	R	V		
Blue-headed Vireo	C	C	U	
Warbling Vireo *	C	C	U	
Philadelphia Vireo	R	R		
Red-eyed Vireo *	C	C	U	
Blue-winged Warbler	R	R	R	
Tennessee Warbler	V	V		
Nashville Warbler	U	U		
Northern Parula	C	C	U	
Yellow Warbler *	C	C	C	
Chestnut-sided Warbler	U	U	V	
Magnolia Warbler	U	U		
Black-th'd Blue Warbler	U	U	U	
Yellow-rumped Warbler	C	C	C	R
Black-th'd Green Warbler	U	U		
Blackburnian Warbler	U	U	R	
Wilson's Warbler	R	R	R	
Pine Warbler	R	R	R	
Prairie Warbler	R	R	R	
Palm Warbler	U	U	U	
Blackpoll Warbler	C	C	U	
Black and White Warbler	U	U	U	
American Redstart *	C	R	C	
Worm-eating Warbler	V	R		
Ovenbird	U		U	
Northern Waterthrush	U	R	U	
Louisiana Waterthrush	R	V		
Kentucky Warbler	U	R	R	
Mourning Warbler	V	V		
Common Yellowthroat *	C	C	C	
Hooded Warbler	C	C	R	
Canada Warbler	R	R	R	
Connecticut Warbler	V	V		
Orange-Crowned Warbler	R	R		
Yellow-breasted Chat	R	R	R	
Eastern Bluebird	R	R	R	V
Cape May Warbler	R	R	R	V
Lincoln's Sparrow	R	R		

Species	Sp	Su	F	W
Scarlet Tanager	U		U	
Northern Cardinal *	C	C	C	C
Rose-breasted Grosbeak	U	V	A	C
Indigo Bunting *	C	C	U	
Rufous-sided Towhee	U		U	
Chipping Sparrow *	C	C	C	R
Field Sparrow	U		U	
Fox Sparrow	U		U	R
Song Sparrow *	A	A	A	C
Swamp Sparrow	U		U	
White-thr'd Sparrow	C		C	C
Dark-eyed Junco	C		A	A
Red-winged Blackbird	U	U	U	U
Common Grackle *	C	C	C	R
Brown-headed Cowbird *	C	C	C	R
Orchard Oriole *	R	R		
Baltimore Oriole *	C	U	R	
Purple Finch	R		R	R
House Finch *	C	C	C	U
Pine Siskin	R		R	R
American Goldfinch *	C	C	A	A
Evening Grosbeak	V		V	V
House Sparrow *	U	U	U	U
White-crowned Sparrow	U		U	R
Savannah Sparrow	R		R	

KEY:

Sp = Spring: March – May
Su = Summer: June – August
F = Fall: September – November
W = Winter: December – February
A = Abundant
C = Common
U = Uncommon
R = Rare
V = Very rare
* = breeds or has bred in cemetery
^ = frequently seen flying overhead

rev. 2-2015

Figure 3.7. Partial list of bird species documented at West Laurel Hill and Cynwyd Heritage Trail.
Source: Gregg Gorton.

or it may be held on a particular day when volunteers all over the country (and, increasingly, the world) gather to document birds. For example, the National Audubon Society held its 115th annual Christmas Bird Count in 2014, and that event is now occurring globally. In 1993, the New Haven (Connecticut) Bird Club established what has become an international bird count called "The Big Sit!" where participants remain within a seventeen-foot-diameter circle and count every bird species they see or hear during a twenty-four-hour time frame. Another example is the Great Backyard Bird Count (held in February), a four-day bird-counting event during which information is gathered to help the National Audubon Society and the Cornell Lab of Ornithology monitor bird populations across the country.

Three cemeteries taking different approaches to effectively educate their visitors about birds are Historic Woodlawn Cemetery in Toledo, Ohio; Historic Oakwood Cemetery in Raleigh, North Carolina; and the Woodlands in Philadelphia. Historic Woodlawn is one of nine sites included in the Oak Openings Loop of the Lake Erie Birding Trail, and it is the only cemetery that is part of this trail. A remarkable 208 species of birds have been found on or near the cemetery grounds.[12] In addition to hosting bird walks, birders meet every Friday to document the birds of Woodlawn, submitting their findings to eBird.org, an online checklist program run by the Cornell Lab of Ornithology. In Raleigh, Historic Oakwood has its own bluebird trail. In conjunction with the North Carolina Bluebird Society, thirteen bluebird boxes were placed throughout the cemetery. Volunteers maintain a spreadsheet as to when the babies hatch and fledge and take their first flight, and cemetery managers can then schedule maintenance activities so as not to interfere with or disturb the breeding birds (e.g., not cutting the grass around the bluebird box when breeding is ongoing). In addition to the trail, the bluebirds are incorporated in many cemetery tours and will be featured as part of the North Carolina Science Festival in a program titled "The Birds and Bees of Oakwood Cemetery." The Woodlands, meanwhile, has turned birding into a competition with its "Birding Smackdown" event, in which it competes with Bartram's Garden, the oldest surviving botanical garden in America, to count the most bird species within a one-week period. Bird-related events are held throughout the week, and the results are posted on the cemetery's website.

Photography

Tourists, amateur photographers, and anyone with a camera phone can be drawn to the beauty, history, and symbolism of cemeteries. While cemeteries usually informally accept or invite the public to take photographs, creating an evening photography program can provide photographers with

Figure 3.8.   Lunar stroll at Laurel Hill Cemetery.
Source: Photo by Emma Stern.

access to an unusual setting, the cemetery at sunset or under a full moon. At Laurel Hill Cemetery, these programs have proven successful enough to require capping the number of participants. Riverside Cemetery in Macon, Georgia, has had success with its "Full Moon Euphoria," where photography sessions are held in conjunction with the full moon.

Here are a few suggestions for organizing a night photography session, whether it is organized by a cemetery or a photography club.

1. For clubs and outside organizations, get permission from the cemetery!
2. Consider having participants sign a waiver.
3. Decide whether the event will coincide with a lunar event or merely be held at night during a temperate time of year.
4. If the event will be in conjunction with a full moon, scout out good locations to view the rising moon.
5. Survey the cemetery grounds for interesting sites or sculptures. These may include a nighttime view of a city vista or a monument that takes on a new appearance in the nighttime light.
6. Reach out to local professional photographers. Professional assistance is needed to advise on camera settings and equipment, as well as assisting amateurs or beginner photographers with setting up shots.
7. Limit the size of the group. Doing so not only helps to control and regroup but also makes it possible for every participant to receive

Figure 3.9.   Laurel Hill Cemetery's ghostly circus.
Source: Photo by Carter Smith.

      instruction when needed. Consider holding a session for beginners
and one for more advanced practitioners.

8. Ask for permission to use the photographs for future event advertising.

Cemeteries for the Performing Arts

In addition to recreational activities focusing on physical activities and
hobbies, cemeteries are becoming popular venues for performances of theater, music, and poetry. Theatre groups and dance troupes are regular performers in cemeteries across the country, and the most successful of these
events often tie them to the space in some way. Perhaps the performance
is inspired by the cemetery, connects to the cycles of life and death, or was
written by someone buried in the cemetery. Along with the performance,
event programmers might include a tour of performing artists buried in the
cemetery. While the backdrop of the burial ground is certainly a unique
setting for a play, poetry reading, or other performance, connecting with
the space can help mitigate any possible negative criticism.

      Cemeteries are also becoming popular spots for concerts, some with
names like "Tunes from the Tombs" and "Music among the Memorials."
Once again, a unique and peaceful setting may be enough to attract visitors,
but making a connection to the cemetery and the deceased buried there can
be a way to justify the program to those unfamiliar with cemetery program-

ming. Movie nights are also gaining in popularity in cemeteries across the country. Laurel Hill Cemetery has been showing movies for the past few years; Green-Wood in Brooklyn has a Silent Night event where silent films featuring cemetery scenes are screened; and Hartford's Cedar Hill Cemetery (the burial place of Katharine Hepburn) offers a movie night featuring one of her films. A movie night is certainly not practical for many cemeteries, but it does offer another way to enjoy recreation amid the dead.

Picnics, Parties, and Egg Hunts: Other Types of Recreation

As centralized community spaces, cemeteries can be used as alternative venues for hosting community or holiday-related events. While a cemetery might strike many as an odd place for an egg hunt, West Laurel Hill Cemetery has successfully drawn hundreds of children to its annual hunt, which has grown tremendously over the past fifteen years. Thousands of candy- or toy-filled plastic eggs are placed in open areas in the cemetery (areas with few or no burials, or only large mausoleums). The day features art activities, entertainers such as balloon artists and jugglers, and of course, photos with the Easter Bunny. The safe and timely flow of traffic, parents, and children is crucial, and advanced planning is a must. Logistics for an event like this can be a challenge, but there have been surprisingly few complaints or questions about holding this event near the graves of the deceased. If considering holding an egg hunt:

- Space considerations are extremely important. Even those parents willing to take their child to an egg hunt held in a cemetery could be concerned if the hunt is held over the graves of the dead. Look for open areas first, or areas were only a few monuments stand.
- Have different areas set aside for different age groups. Preventing ten-year-olds and two-year-olds from competing for eggs will allow all of the children to take home treats.
- Organize prehunt activities and entertainment such as magicians, jugglers, or arts and crafts to keep the children occupied prior to the start of the event.
- Look for sponsors. Approach local confection companies for donations of candy.

In the nineteenth century, Americans would picnic or stroll in the rural cemeteries. Today, as Americans begin to embrace the return of alternate uses of cemeteries, one activity that is making a comeback is the Sunday cemetery picnic. A number of cemeteries have created annual events offering entertainment, food, vendors, and tours. Historic Oakland Cemetery in Atlanta has been holding its Sunday in the Park event for more than thirty-five years. The event features multiple stages, food trucks, carriage and walking tours, and a costume contest for Victorian-era garb. Organizations can also attract visitors by simply holding an open house. Opening the cemetery one night a week in the summer can attract joggers, bicyclists, or dog walkers interested in exercising after the peak heat of the summer day.

Conclusion

Whether the cemetery itself is organizing the event or a community organization is looking for a venue, burial grounds can be a great choice for recreational activities. Both the community and cemetery staff should consider these essential questions before developing any such programming:

1. Is the cemetery open and available for recreational use?
2. Does cemetery management/ownership approve of alternative uses?
3. What liability issues might arise as a result of holding recreational activities in the cemetery, and is the cemetery adequately protected?
4. Is the cemetery listed on local, regional, or national recreation or walking trail lists?
5. Are there local, state, or national recreational events the cemetery can participate in?
6. What local partnerships can be developed to help attract visitors?

Notes

1. Downing, *Rural Essays*, 144.
2. Laurel Hill Cemetery, "Meeting of the Managers, January 19th, 1844."
3. Smith, *Smith's Illustrated Guide to and Through Laurel Hill Cemetery*, 38.
4. National Recreation Trails, http://americantrails.org/nationalrecreation trails.
5. Loving, "Heel; Sit; Stay; Roll Over—and Don't Walk on the Graves," 14.
6. Old City Cemetery, www.gravegarden.org.
7. Friends of Mount Auburn, "Ornithologists and Benefactors of Birds at Mount Auburn," 5.
8. Pearson, *The Bird Study Book*, 227.
9. Downing, *The Nature-Study Review*, 302.
10. National Humane Review, "The Largest Cemetery Bird Sanctuary in America," 152.
11. Carver, *Birding in the United States*, 4.
12. Woodlawn Cemetery and Arboretum, http://www.historic-woodlawn .com/birds.html.

Reflection

4

Programming Ceremony

> *Here it will be in the power of every one, who may wish it, at an expense considerably less than that of a common tomb, or a vault beneath a church, to deposit the mortal remains of his friends, and to provide a place of burial for himself, which, while living, he may contemplate without dread or disgust; one which is secure from the danger of being encroached upon, as in the graveyards of the city; secluded from every species of uncongenial intrusion; surrounded with everything that can fill the heart with tender and respectful emotions; beneath the shade of a venerable tree, on the slope of the verdant lawn, and within the seclusion of the forest; removed from all the discordant scenes of life.*[1]

—"The Proposed Rural Cemetery." by Hon. Edward Everett

Even today, cemeteries are created to serve dual purposes. They provide a service to society by disposing of the dead in a sanitary and efficient way. Beyond their utility, however, lies another function. They act as liminal spaces. Cemeteries both isolate the dead and allow for a space to commune with them. They keep the dead alive through memorialization, but at the same time they confine these dead bodies to a permanent and fixed place. Cemeteries fulfill a need many Americans are unaware they have by providing a place for reconnection, meditation, and contemplation. While there are other, more efficient, ways to dispose of the dead (both in terms of resources consumed and time and ease of disposal), Americans continue to bury and memorialize their loved ones in individually marked graves.

Even cremated remains are frequently buried in ground or inurned in a niche, while some progressive cemeteries are establishing scattering gardens for environmentally conscious or simplicity-minded consumers. Green or natural burial grounds, which have become more popular in America as the twenty-first century progresses, usually offer a type of memorial, whether it be a natural marker, digital memorial, tree, or plant. Increasing numbers of Americans would like to be buried without contaminating the earth with metal and concrete, but often they, too, hope to be visited in death, and hold the expectation of memorialization.

Not only traditional burials, then, but all methods of disposal of the dead provide an opportunity for a permanent memorial—and offer the living a place to go to in order to reconnect with the deceased. In this way, cemeteries are by their very nature places for reflection. If Americans were concerned merely with the disposal of the dead, there would be no monuments, inscriptions, art, or nature to welcome visitors. There would be no benches or pathways to access graves. There would be no mementoes left at monuments to show the deceased is remembered and visited. Similarly, the very act of creating and executing cemetery programming is a form of reflection. By telling the stories of those from our past, we are both remembering them and seeing them through contemporary eyes. By relaying their stories, ours can take on new meanings. We can examine and remember in order to better understand our world and our place within it.

Figure 4.1.   Confederates decorate graves in Hollywood Cemetery, 1867.
Source: Library of Congress Prints and Photographs Division.

Historical Context

Up until the 1830s, burial grounds were not places to visit to contemplate the meaning of life or remember lost loved ones. They were places to be avoided entirely. Shallow burials, frequent disinterments, neglect, and vandalism all contributed to dismal and foul-smelling graveyards. Edward Everett, politician, orator, and supporter for the founding of Mount Auburn Cemetery, created an address to be published in the Boston newspapers in which he criticized the city's burial grounds for, among other things, appearances "as little calculated as possible to invite the visits of the seriously disposed."[2]

The founders of Mount Auburn and the other early rural cemeteries viewed these new creations as places for contemplation and escape from the "harassing din"[3] of the cities, where increased industrialization was creating an atmosphere of noise, dirt, and crowds. At the same time, the dead, for the first time in American history, would be isolated from the living community. Where burial grounds had once been at the center of New England towns (both to protect the bodies from disturbance from wild animals and as a puritanical reminder of the constant presence of death), the establishment of Mount Auburn would now push burials out to the countryside. Burial grounds would no longer stand in the way of the "progress" of commerce and industrialization; the establishment of rural cemeteries would minimize the risk of new building construction disturbing the bones of ancestors. Moreover, the dead could now be remembered when it was convenient, with visits scheduled into a busy life. The romantic landscape could counterbalance the developing city, and with a simple carriage ride across the Charles River, a Bostonian could meditate or attempt to gain perspective on life, protected from the noise and pressures of a growing city. Visitors could visit the cemetery not only to "recuperate from modernity" but also to "rethink their role in it,"[4] protected by the quiet, natural environment.

The idea of using the mortality reflected in a cemetery to contemplate life, as embraced by the founders of Mount Auburn, was very much tied into Victorian ideas of romanticism, nature, and melancholy—and was vastly different from previous views held by New Englanders. The strict Calvinism of the past had yielded to Universalist beliefs, and this, along with the development of Romanticism in America, radically altered views regarding nature. While Calvinist thinking saw nature as an adversary, the Bostonians of the early nineteenth century were better able to accept the ideas of nature as a blessing. The presence of nature in the cemetery was thought to exert a positive influence on those visiting the graves of loved ones. Nature was no longer something to be feared, but celebrated. It would help to soothe and comfort those experiencing loss.

These thoughts appear frequently in the rhetoric used to talk about Mount Auburn. In his speech "A Discourse on the Burial of the Dead," physician and cemetery founder Jacob Bigelow observes, "The scenes which, under most other circumstances, are repulsive and disgusting, are by the joint influence of nature and art rendered beautiful, attractive, and consoling."[5] Nature could help to transform thoughts of grief. In *Mount Auburn: Its Scenes, Its Beauties, and Its Lessons*, the naturalist Wilson Flagg notes how visiting the dead in the setting of nature can result in transcendent thoughts. "We come here not to be saddened, but to be sobered; to think more earnestly of the higher purposes of life."[6] By burying their dead in a place like Mount Auburn, Bostonions not only would be better able to deal with the grief associated with death but also would be "agreeably affected" by the beauty of nature.[7]

The establishment of the nineteenth-century rural cemeteries also coincided with and led to the creation of some of the country's first tribute or commemorative memorials. Even before the establishment of Mount Auburn, for example, cemetery advocates had proposed erecting a monument in honor of George Washington.[8] Upon completion of the cemetery, Washington Tower was built on a summit overlooking the Charles River. Memorials like the Washington Tower frequently were (and remain) focal points and landmarks within a cemetery, sharing "the common objective of perpetuating the memory or ideals" of the organization erecting them.[9] Just as burial grounds were seen as evidence of colonized land, these monuments attempted to legitimize the actions of the political body in control by "glorifying the remains of figures whose significance reflects the principles and mission of the nation."[10] A tribute monument is also a way to address deaths occurring in a faraway place where, perhaps, the body has never been recovered. This became especially clear with the development of the Civil War, which saw scores of Americans dying far from their homes.

The establishment of the rural cemetery also began the transition away from church-controlled burial grounds to more secular spaces where the dead were united by place and economic background rather than by religion. To be sure, churches would continue to exert control over burial of the dead (and continue to control some cemeteries today), but the 1830s saw the beginning of a transition away from solely clergy-controlled memorialization to a new corporate-controlled design. This transition was eased, in part, by the location of the new cemeteries. For example, in the nineteenth century, it would have taken between an hour and a half and two hours to get from the center of Philadelphia to Laurel Hill

Cemetery. Established far away from the churches and church-controlled burial grounds, the cemetery was not founded with the clergy in mind.[11] Cemetery managers created a sacred space of their own by separating it from the profane space, controlling access to the cemetery and developing the equivalent of a "formal cult of the saints" by publishing guidebooks featuring well-known ancestors buried within the cemetery.[12] The public (with guidance and restrictions from cemetery management) could choose the symbols and memorials to best reflect their belief in the afterlife. The cemetery, not the clergy, would control how and when the public commemorated their loved ones.

In the twenty-first century, Americans are even more in need of a place for quiet contemplation. In a cemetery, a visitor can choose to "unplug" from the constant noise and disruptions found in everyday life and reconnect with something greater than themselves. Whether one seeks religious or spiritual communion or merely the sense of being both alone and part of a larger connected universe, the peace and quiet found in cemeteries is a welcome break from the noise, pace, and bustle of life.

Remembrance Programming

While a cemetery visit on holidays and special occasions is not the prescribed behavior it once was, Americans still perform rituals of mourning and remembrance connected to cemeteries. Visiting a cemetery is a chance to set aside time to remember. It is an accepted way to process grief. Holidays such as Christmas, Easter, Memorial Day, and Mother's Day are still popular times to leave wreaths, flowers, or grave decorations behind. Those unable to physically visit have wreaths, flowers, or greeting cards delivered to the gravesite. In the Jewish tradition, a formal unveiling ceremony is scheduled in the cemetery to coincide with the setting of the memorial. During this ceremony (which typically occurs before the Yahrzeit or anniversary of death) the gravestone is wrapped in cloth and formally unveiled to the gathered family members. It is a time for the family to come together and remember the deceased.

A cemetery can develop programming surrounding the widespread need to hold a ceremony or formal event to remember the dead. As Americans have become disconnected with the religious and cultural institutions that once guided mourning rituals, and the orthodoxy governing mourning has relaxed, a cemetery can partially fill that void by offering opportunities (and the setting) for these ceremonies to occur. While not everyone needs rituals to process grief, many others would welcome the opportunity to remember the dead with ceremony and ritual not necessarily tied to their own religious or ethnic tradition(s).

A wreath-laying ceremony is one popular way to honor the dead. The laurel wreath is an ancient symbol representing the circle of eternal life or immortality, because the leaves of the laurel do not wilt.[13] The act of leaving a graveside tribute—whether the memento is traditional (like flowers or visiting stones) or specific to the deceased (golf balls at Bobby Jones's grave or pennies at the plot of John Wilkes Booth)—serves to honor the departed and, perhaps, bring good luck to the visitor. Visiting a cemetery and seeing someone's gravestone still holds meaning and helps us connect with that individual. The objects we bring with us to the cemetery can help make that relationship seem concrete.

In terms of cemetery programming, a common and popular event to remember those who have died is an annual memorial service, sometimes held in conjunction with All Souls' Day. Such services are opportunities to remember loved ones who have died and honor them with a tribute or ceremony. Cemeteries could choose to read the names of those who died or were buried within the past year, have the event officiated by clergy, or perform a candle-lighting ceremony. The objective of a memorial service is to take time to remember those who are gone and reflect on the lives they lived. In West Laurel Hill Cemetery, a cemetery where memorial services date back to the 1930s, families return year after year to honor their family members. This Annual Memorial Service, held every fall, has become a simple but important way for attendees to acknowledge and remember family they've lost.

In Christian cemeteries, Easter is another annual event used for inspiration, remembrance, and commemoration. Just as spring is a time of rebirth and renewal, services held on Easter are opportunities to move forward and celebrate the belief that the dead live on. By commemorating the dead, we are placing them in a confined space, acknowledging that life continues and reinforcing the need to keep living. Remembrance programming becomes a life-affirming community event where rituals serve both to honor and remember the dead, but more importantly acknowledge the continuance of life.

Anniversaries connected with tragic events are also times when a community can be united through remembrance programming. Recent events such as the September 11th attacks have led to annual ceremonies at cemeteries across the country. Local tragedies also generate a need within communities to pause and remember. Anniversaries of international tragedies, such as the one-hundredth anniversary of the Armenian genocide, can also be remembered in American cemeteries, especially those connected through shared cultures, ethnicities, or ancestral lineage. While the descendants of victims might not have a formal place to go to honor and remember, cemeteries, as perceived sacred spaces, are logical choices for commemoration and memorial programs. These ceremonies help individuals remember and honor the dead while educating and uniting the community. They also serve to reinforce and instill the community's values in the next generation.

Veterans and Patriotic Programming

When the first rural cemeteries were founded in the 1830s, Americans were wrestling with how to lay claim to their heritage. With no great tradition of public monuments and the last of the Revolutionary War veterans dying, civic leaders felt the absence of statues and monuments to communicate and instill patriotism in the next generation. Edward Everett articulated this concern in his address advocating for the establishment of Mount Auburn: "The mother of Washington lies buried in a field, the property of a person not related to her family, and in a spot which cannot now be identified."[14] Everett, Bigelow, and others hoped that walking through Mount Auburn and passing the graves of people like John Hooton—a soldier in the Revolutionary War and participant in the Boston Tea Party—would foster a greater awareness of history, reinvigorate patriotism, and nurture a system of social roots linking present and past generations.

Cemeteries did, in fact, become places to honor veterans. Early monuments noted their contributions while ceremonies on holidays such as Decoration Day (established following the Civil War) and later Memorial Day featured parades, speakers, and gatherings of veterans. Memorial Day and Veterans Day services can still be found in cemeteries across the country, and holding these ceremonies in a cemetery is a logical choice. Not only do cemeteries provide close physical proximity to the dead buried beneath our feet, they are viewed as sacred spaces. Events can range from a simple wreath-laying ceremony to a more elaborate tribute with speeches, parades, music, and gun salutes.

Cemetery veteran-oriented programming can also provide an opportunity to partner with schools and civic organizations on volunteer opportunities. Students looking for a Martin Luther King Jr. Day of Service project can be charged with placing American flags at the graves of veterans. The program "Wreaths across America" coordinates wreath-laying ceremonies across America on a specific Saturday each December. Today's ceremonies serve purposes similar to those of their historical predecessors, uniting communities and helping visitors both remember and reflect on death and loss. They assist in socializing the younger generation by indicating which events and deeds the community has chosen to remember with monuments, memorials, and ceremony. By confining mourning to a designated time and place, these ceremonies also create a safe space for expressing public emotion and connecting with the dead.

Anniversaries and birthdays provide additional occasions for cemeteries to coordinate special events and programming connected with veterans. For the 150th anniversary of the end of the Civil War, Green-Wood Cemetery placed a candle at the grave of every Civil War veteran buried in the cemetery. Nearly five thousand veterans were honored with a procession led by uniformed reenactors, cavalry horses, and musicians. Establishing a cemetery event on the birthday of a well-known leader is both an opportunity to honor individual accomplishments and to connect to broader contemporary themes. Laurel Hill Cemetery and the General George Meade Society (a Philadelphia-based organization dedicated to preserving the memory of the general) hold an annual champagne toast honoring Meade on his birthday.

Figure 4.2.   General Meade Society honors George Meade at Laurel Hill.
Source: Photo by Emma Stern.

U.S. presidents receive a wreath on their birthdays, sent, tradition holds, by the current sitting president. Many cemeteries where their remains reside hold a memorial service in conjunction with the event. Even Jefferson Davis, the president of the Confederacy, is honored with an annual memorial service at his final resting place in Hollywood Cemetery in Richmond, Virginia. Members of the Jefferson F. Davis Memorial Committee, an entity of the Sons of Confederate Veterans, use his birthday as an opportunity to honor not only the man but also "southern ancestors and their leaders." In this way, a defined birthday celebration is used to more broadly celebrate and remember local and regional history and values.

Here is a list of suggested steps to start veteran-related programming in a community cemetery:

1. Form partnerships. Organizations such as the American Legion, Boy Scouts, and Daughters of the American Revolution are often willing volunteers for commemorating veterans and will help promote and lend their attendance to the event. They also might maintain records and lists of local veterans and their burial places. A partnership with a local historical society can be used to create an exhibit complementing an anniversary service.
2. Research veterans. Maintain an active list of veterans by war, branch, and/or special contributions or awards.
3. Document and mark veteran graves. Often, volunteers can place flags at the graves of veterans. Maintaining a list of veterans can make the process easier, and the placement of these flags is a striking visual tribute.
4. Organize events to coincide with anniversaries relating to battles or the start or end of a war. Ceremonies held on the anniversary of special events are opportunities to reach a broader audience.
5. Tell individual stories. Conduct walking tours highlighting the cemetery's general military history, or specialized tours focusing on a branch of the armed services or Medal of Honor recipients. Look to tell the stories of buried soldiers to help visitors establish a greater understanding of the roles of individuals in a great conflict.
6. Offer to hold local ceremonies inside the cemetery. Ceremonies generally occurring in municipal parks can often be more effective by moving among the graves of the honored deceased.

Case Study: Duffy's Cut and West Laurel Hill Cemetery

As permanent repositories of memorials, cemeteries have opportunities to unite a community by offering a tangible place to gather to remember a person or group of people whose lives helped to shape the world we live in today. Sometimes the memorial or cenotaph merely serves as a physical reminder of individuals whose bodies could not be found or reburied. In the case of the Duffy's Cut memorial, a cemetery unconnected with historical events serves as a place for a permanent memorial and a place of remembrance, community connection, and ethnic identification.

The Duffy's Cut tragedy dates to 1832. Scores of Irish laborers were coming to America and helping to build the nation and its infrastructure. Fifty-seven Irish Catholic workers were hired to build a section of the Pennsylvania Railroad, west of the city of Philadelphia, referred to as Duffy's Cut. While the exact circumstances of their deaths remain unclear, cholera spread among the workers, but community prejudice against the immigrants eventually led to violence and contributed to the demise of the entire group. It was only in the early part of the twenty-first century that an archeological dig helped retrieve the bodies, which were buried in a

Figure 4.3.   Duffy's Cut remembrance ceremony, 2012.
Source: Duffy's Cut Project.

mass grave, and to document the people's lives and deaths. For the bodies and bones retrieved (and in a few cases identified), project leaders looked for a suitable site to lay the remains to rest. West Laurel Hill Cemetery, although not in existence at the time of the tragedy, donated the gravesite and memorial. The annual ceremony honoring victims has turned into an important event for the general community and for Irish ancestry groups such as the Donegal Society, not just to remember the victims but also to commemorate the workers who built America. While the bones of most of the victims will likely never be retrieved (they are partially buried under a train line), the placement and ceremony represents something greater than those few bodies buried there. It represents community, heritage, and sacrifice. Holding the event and placing the monument in a cemetery preserves the memorial itself as well as the memory of those who rest beneath it.

Other Types of Reflection Programming

Across the country, cemeteries and organizations using cemeteries are beginning to consider types of programming that, while ceremonial or reflective in nature, are not traditional cemetery activities. Mount Auburn Cemetery held a program on "situational awareness" in which participants learned to use nature to heal and revive their spirits. Other nontraditional activities include death cafés and weddings. The common factor is the recognition of the cemetery as a transcendent place, an optimal setting to address profound questions or to celebrate extraordinary events and milestones in a person's life.

Death Cafés

Entering a cemetery prepares most individuals, at least on some level, to think about death. A topic that is taboo or unpopular in most places is accepted conversational material within a cemetery. For these reasons, cemeteries have become popular locations for death cafés, a concept that originated in Europe in 2011 but has since spread and become popular in America. The event is an open forum where people can have conversations about death. The first cemetery in the country to host a death café was Historic Oakland in Atlanta, Georgia. Oakland's cafes have been so successful that the cemetery has hosted twenty such events in the two years since the program's inception.

In many ways, a cemetery is ideally suited for sensitive discussions about death. Entering a cemetery places death in the forefront of one's mind. Frequently filled with beautiful art and architecture and trees and plantings, the cemetery provides a setting that helps soothe anxiety. Conversations traditionally held for the first time in hospitals or under trying circumstances seem less threatening when held in a place of beauty; death seems less harsh and ugly. Little is needed for a cemetery to host a death café other than a space to accommodate a group of people, a host, and a willingness to hold open, sensitive conversations. The death café website, www.deathcafe.com, offers guidelines for holding such an event.

Weddings

Holding a wedding ceremony in a cemetery? It strikes most as an incongruous thought, but Mount Auburn, Green-Wood, Laurel Hill and West Laurel Hill, Spring Grove (Cincinnati), Historic Oakland (Atlanta), Lakeview Cemetery (Cleveland, Ohio) and Mountain View Cemetery (Oakland, California) are among the cemeteries that regularly hold weddings and market such opportunities to the general public. While a small percentage of couples are looking for Goth or Halloween-themed ceremonies, most are merely looking for a picturesque setting. Some ceremonies are held in chapels on the cemetery grounds, while others take place in front of large, private mausoleums or in a particularly scenic spot in the cemetery. Many of the couples that choose a cemetery are looking for a unique location, perhaps a setting with interesting statues and architecture and gorgeous trees. They appreciate the *space* of the cemetery without the ties of sadness or loss.

Conclusion

Cemeteries already have credibility as places for remembrance. They have been and will continue to be informally used as places to reflect, remember, and reconnect to the past. Developing remembrance programming is often less challenging than convincing a community to use a cemetery for nontraditional purposes.

Looking to use your local cemetery for remembrance programming?

1. Look at what other organizations are already doing and figure out ways for those ceremonies or programs to occur in your cemetery.
2. Use service organizations and volunteer programs as partners.
3. Be willing to consider nontraditional or "out-of-the-box" programs.
4. Start with the basics by holding an annual memorial service or Memorial Day tribute.

Case Study 4.1: Death, Reflection, and Culture: The Dia de los Muertos Project

Overview

Laurel Hill is the first cemetery in the nation to be recognized as a National Historic Landmark and is a unique resource for the local communities that it serves. With over seventy-five thousand permanent residents buried throughout seventy-eight acres of land, there are unlimited themes to draw upon and countless stories to be told. In addition to year-round public programming, the cemetery offers customized private tours and activities for both students and adults. The program outlined below was developed for a group of fifth-, sixth-, and seventh-graders from a local elementary school when their teacher reached out about scheduling a tour of the cemetery during the Halloween season. We worked together to create a unique program that aimed to teach history, art, and cultural understanding through the context of Laurel Hill Cemetery.

How to Create a Dia de los Muertos Event

ACTIVITIES

Before the visit, make sure to plan ahead and schedule plenty of volunteers and chaperones to assist with the activities. Upon arrival, split the students into two groups to complete their activities. Group size should be no more than fifteen to twenty students, if possible. Group A will begin their visit with a guided walking tour of Laurel Hill's historic grounds, while Group B completes the Dia de los Muertos Art Project. After approximately one hour, the two groups will meet at the central gatehouse area and switch activities. The groups may meet again after two hours for an optional picnic lunch on the grounds.

GUIDED WALKING TOUR

During the tour component of the program, instruct the guide to point out some of the most notable art, architecture, symbolism, and individuals in the cemetery. Consult with the teacher ahead of time to find out what students are currently learning in class. For example, if they are studying earth science, the guide might point out specific examples of how granite and marble weather over time. In addition to history, art, and architecture, the cemetery is a great place to incorporate lessons in science and nature.

While on the grounds, students usually have many questions about what lies beneath their feet. One of the most commonly asked questions is: "Are we stepping on someone?" During a recent tour a guide overheard an eighth-grader mumbling to the headstones, "Excuse me, sorry about that!" as he attempted to jump over the graves. It's important for guides to answer general questions about cemeteries and death openly and honestly. Quite frequently kids will ask questions about death that many adults are not comfortable asking, or are too polite to bring up, such as how the person died and what happens to the body once it goes into the ground. Many students are also curious to learn about biographies, headstone markings, family plots, and the ages of the deceased. Laurel Hill is the final resting place of numerous notables, including Philadelphia's leading industrialists, Civil War generals, artists, inventors, writers, and entertainers. It is home to many average citizens as well. By answering questions about who rests beneath the earth they're walking on, students are not only taught about Philadelphia history but also how the narratives of the deceased have shaped society today and how it connects to their own lives.

Dia de los Muertos (The Day of the Dead) Art Project

The Mexican national holiday Dia de los Muertos is a time for the living to gather and honor those who have died. There are many traditions associated with the holiday, including visiting cemeteries and churchyards, building colorful, elaborate altars, and preparing favorite foods of the deceased. Marigolds are the traditional flower used to honor the dead and are often placed on gravesites and in altars alongside decorative skulls made out of sugar or clay. The celebration is filled with rich and colorful imagery and is not meant to be morose, rendering it a fitting theme for a student project.

- Begin with a brief background of the holiday, such as traditional customs and how they connect to the cemetery.
- Supply an array of colorful squares of tissue paper and pipe cleaners. Layer two or three squares of different colored paper, and fold them accordion style. Tie a pipe cleaner around the center of the paper accordion. Then carefully peel up each individual tissue layer and shape it until it forms a circle. Your paper marigold is complete.
- Ask each student to write the name of someone they'd like to honor on a piece of paper and tie it to the pipe cleaner stem of their paper marigold. Namesakes may include living or deceased ancestors, friends, pets, famous people, or individuals buried at Laurel Hill.

- Create your own skull template or download one from the web. Print out a few versions so that there are several options for students to choose from. This will make the installation as a whole look more unique. Pass out the templates and have students decorate their paper skulls with paint, markers, stickers, glitter, and other items. You may want to precut the skulls to save time. You can also punch holes in the sides and use a string to make a festive take-home mask.
- Take a moment for reflection, and ask for volunteers to share who they chose to remember and why. Display the projects along a line with clothespins in a central location to create a festive "ofrenda," or altar of remembrance. Give students the choice to leave their creations behind, or take them home at the end of the visit. Leave the installation up for the remainder of the day for visitors to enjoy and photograph.

Response

For many students on the trip, it was their first visit to a cemetery. Overall, they seemed to enjoy their time at Laurel Hill and gained an understanding

Figure 4.4.   Dia de los Muertos, Laurel Hill Cemetery.
Source: Emma Stern.

of how cemeteries can be used as places of learning for history, art, science, and outdoor recreation. The teachers and parents had just as much fun as the students. After the program, they wrote brief field studies about their experiences at Laurel Hill that were published in the school's newsletter. The school booked a visit with us for the following year, and students have returned with their parents for other programs and events.

Emma Stern is the director of programs at the Laurel Hill Cemetery.

Notes

1. Bigelow, *A History of Mt. Auburn Cemetery*, 138–39.
2. Bigelow, *A History of Mt. Auburn Cemetery*, 137.
3. Bigelow, *A History of Mt. Auburn Cemetery*, 195.
4. Sachs, *Arcadian America*, 55.
5. Bigelow, *A History of Mt. Auburn Cemetery*, 194.
6. Flagg, *Mount Auburn*, 36.
7. Flagg, *Mount Auburn*, 34.
8. Linden, *Silent City on a Hill*, 228.
9. McDowell and Meyer, *The Revival Styles in American Memorial Art*, 4.
10. Laderman, *The Sacred Remains*, 6.
11. McDannell, *Material Christianity*, 110.
12. McDannell, *Material Christianity*, 111–13.
13. Keister, *Stories in Stone*, 48.
14. Bigelow, *A History of Mt. Auburn Cemetery*, 138.

Marketing Cemetery Programs   **5**

It is not enough merely to create a cemetery tour or innovative program, you must then figure out how to reach potential visitors and bring them into the cemetery. While many historical and cultural institutions grapple with this same challenge, cemeteries bring an added layer of complexity to the discussion. While in the past ten to fifteen years, cemetery tours have become more common across the nation, the general public is still getting acclimated to the idea. Many people hold narrow views of what a cemetery is and can be, and have never even thought to visit a cemetery for a nonfuneral purpose. In fact, some may find it difficult to shake fears and superstitions associated with setting foot in a burial ground.

Recognition of the fact that cemeteries are largely viewed as sacred spaces—and anticipation of the complex emotions that cemetery visits may engender—should be the foundation of any marketing effort. Creating programming the public sees as respectful is essential not only for building an audience but also for maintaining good relationships and avoiding negative press. Those who create events and tours held in cemeteries have to be particularly sensitive to the community they serve and aware of how programming might be received. At the same time, unconventional and even controversial programming can attract both visitors and positive media attention. Conservative programs will only take the cemetery so far, and there are ways to successfully introduce unconventional programming as you attempt to reinvent or reinterpret the cemetery space.

Know Your Potential Audience

The first step in thinking about marketing any kind of cemetery programming is to know your potential audience.

- Look at what's right outside your gates. Who are the cemetery's neighbors? What local businesses or community organizations might have an interest in seeing the cemetery succeed?
- What groups are already using the cemetery—whether formally or informally, for traditional or nontraditional activities? Maybe a local scout troop or American Legion post places flags on the graves of veterans. Possibly a local history organization is already conducting tours. These existing activities are opportunities not only to see how the cemetery can be used for programming but also to evaluate public interest. They also point to groups of people who are already interested in the cemetery and its success, and can be approached for support.
- What organizations are most active in the community, and how might their members be interested in using the cemetery space? Create a list of active groups and assess how their members might support the cemetery. For example, a community service–oriented organization might want to organize a cemetery cleanup day. A garden club could focus on adding new plantings or conducting a horticulture tour. A historical society's members might be interested in surveying the cemetery for genealogical purposes.
- If you are working on behalf of an organization other than the cemetery, what would your group's members be most interested in seeing, learning about, or participating in?

Every cemetery will have different parameters for acceptable programming. Patrons of a nondenominational cemetery in the Northeast and those of a Baptist cemetery in the South are likely to embrace very different sorts of programming. Cemeteries conducting few new burials will be able to take greater risks with edgier marketing than cemeteries that are still very active. Both cemetery staff creating programming and outside organizations interested in using their community cemetery for alternative uses must first know their audience and be sensitive to and respectful of their values.

Start with the Safe

For institutions just beginning to develop programming, starting with "safe" programming can help build a base of support and gauge the community's

Figure 5.1.   Spirits with the Spirits, Elmwood Cemetery.
Source: Shonna Camp-Springer.

reaction to using the cemetery in multidimensional ways. Once you determine who your audience is, you might gradually introduce tours that appeal to your traditional constituency. Safe programming would include memorial services and patriotic events, or a general historic or 101 Tour that introduces basic cemetery history and landmarks. Starting with a general introduction tour will get the public used to the idea of visiting a cemetery for educational purposes.

It can take time to successfully build a roster of diverse programming. In order to minimize negative feedback, it's best to start with the basics. Look at whether your cemetery or local historical organization has ever attempted any kind of programming in the past and what kinds of events have been organized. Annual memorial services and veterans or Memorial Day ceremonies are common across the country. In fact, some cemeteries have been conducting them for decades. These kinds of events can be the foundation to building a more robust programming schedule because they are ceremonial in nature and are still within what the public views as the traditional role of a cemetery.

Once the public becomes more comfortable with cemetery programs, more controversial themes or topics can gradually enter the schedule. In the case of Elmwood Cemetery in Memphis, Tennessee, it took fifteen years of acclimating the public through traditional cemetery tours and programming before staff and administration felt comfortable offering a "Scandals and Scoundrels" tour and a "What a Way to Go" tour (detailing unusual causes of death). These tours, rather than drawing negative feedback, have proven to be among Elmwood's most popular. Recently, Elmwood introduced a "Spirits with the Spirits" gala, held in the cemetery, as another chance to market the space. This yearly event features community sponsorships, an auction, and cocktails, and it acts as a form of marketing by bringing people through the gates.

The process of developing cemetery programming takes time. Build upon preexisting events to start, and gradually introduce new ideas. You'll experience more excitement and openness than you will complaints.

Careful Marketing

Many cemeteries beginning to develop programming do so out of financial necessity. Without adequate income from new sales and burials, there is a need to look for alternative ways to engage the public. For that reason alone, most cemeteries seeking to promote their events will not have a budget sufficient to conduct a great deal of paid or conventional advertising. Fortunately, in the twenty-first century, there are multiple avenues for spreading the word about an event or set of programs.

- Post events on both physical and virtual billboards, newsletters and community calendars, and activity guides. Many of these places will post events at no charge.
- Become part of your community's arts or cultural alliance to reach out to audiences looking for relevant events and programming.
- Find out the dates for special communitywide events, like a First Friday or a museum month, and determine how your organization can participate. Try to develop programs in conjunction with local festivals, holidays, or special occasions. The media is more likely to cover a cemetery event held in conjunction with a broader celebration, garnering free publicity.
- Hold an evening open house or flashlight tour. This is a relatively simple way to bring new people into a cemetery. Most adults have never gone to a cemetery at night. Opening the gates in the evening can introduce a "spooky" atmosphere without the risk of controversy that could come with a Halloween or Day of the Dead event. Historic Oakwood Cemetery in Raleigh, North Carolina, has been conducting evening open houses with great success. They combined them with their First Friday Flashlight Tours that feature different routes highlighting Confederate veterans and mourning art and symbolism. Greenwood Cemetery in Orlando, Florida, began offering a series of moonlight historical walking tours in 2005. Held each month during a full moon, these tours were an effort to reach out to the community following extensive hurricane destruction. The simple act of opening the cemetery at night can prove to be a great draw.
- Create a list of local media contacts and prepare press releases for special tours or events.
- Establish and maintain a consistent social media presence using sites such as Facebook, Twitter, Pinterest, and Instagram.
- Develop an offsite version of an introductory tour. Offer to speak at organizations whose members might most be interested in attending a cemetery event.
- Form partnerships. Reach out to clubs and organizations whose members might be interested in participating in cemetery events, or who might be interested in financial support or sponsorships.
- Establish a mailing list. Gather postal as well as email addresses, if possible, and do your best to keep the list up to date. A mailing

list allows you to advertise future events as well as appeals for membership, donations, and volunteers.

If your cemetery has a newsletter, use that as an opportunity to gather information about community interests. If paper mailings are beyond the scope of your budget, a number of inexpensive email newsletter services allow you to reach members easily. Keep them apprised of upcoming tours and projects at the cemetery. Newsletters can spotlight a particular monument or person. They can be used to entice visitors back to the cemetery through "I spy" contests. Consistent, relevant, and interesting communication keeps visitors engaged and aware of your mission and focus.

- Offer space to local organizations for either an indoor meeting space or outdoor space. Groups are often *looking* for interesting places to conduct poetry readings or hold book clubs. Opening a cemetery to these groups not only helps to bring people through the gates but also creates a base of possible future supporters and programming collaborators, guides, and volunteers.

Both cemeteries and groups creating cemetery tours need to be cognizant of the language and imagery they use when advertising their programming. Keep in mind a few basic guidelines when constructing advertising and marketing materials.

- Promote the history. Successful event marketing should begin with an emphasis on the idea of cemeteries as a permanent repository of a community's history and art.
- Avoid the macabre (at least initially). Even flashlight or full moon tours should attempt to move past the creepy. While touring a cemetery at night naturally creates an atmosphere of eeriness, ghost imagery may alienate as many potential visitors as it attracts.
- After a community becomes acclimated to visiting a cemetery for educational or recreational purposes, it is okay to begin pushing the envelope a bit. Halloween tours in a cemetery can be a tremendous draw. Provocative content on a walking tour will attract audiences. Less conventional themes are more likely to draw media attention. With an established base of visitors or members who understand your mission, you will be more able to take chances with innovative programming.
- Know how to address criticism. No matter how "safe" a cemetery tour attempts to be, someone might be offended. Human emotions are unpredictable, and you can never completely assume what will or will not upset a visitor. The key is to listen to criticism, but more

Figure 5.2. Oakland Halloween tours.
Source: Dan Price, courtesy of the Historic Oakland Foundation.

importantly, to be able to explain why the program fits with the cemetery's mission and how cemetery programming is a form of preservation.

What do you do if your most famous "resident" is not someone whose deeds should be celebrated? What if a monument or inscription is offensive to large groups of visitors? How do you navigate the delicate terrain between noting someone's life and works and glorifying them by ignoring their flaws? Travel to almost any cemetery south of the Mason Dixon line and these questions appear front and center. Southern cemeteries, some of which were founded to bury the Confederate dead, face a constant evaluation of how to tell these stories, but their struggles are familiar to anyone who attempts to evaluate the past through the eyes of the present.

As humans, we are complex creatures. We are capable of great achievements just as easily as we are of great destruction. And these two impulses coexist. So how does a cemetery programmer address a well-known figure without ignoring his flaws? Whether it is an industrialist who made his fortune exploiting cheap labor or a well-known Confederate general who also was a leader in the KKK, all cemeteries have complicated figures buried within their walls, because humans are complicated. Every institution has to reconcile dissonant perspectives, and what might be fitting for one institution may not work for another.

- Consider your audience. Who are they and where are they from? Are they locals or tourists? Will addressing a controversy detract from the message and alienate the group?
- "Embrace complexity" by understanding that dualities exist. Someone who is beloved as a local community founder might also have been a bigoted racist. And just as we evolve as a society, our understanding of the past changes based on the present.[1]
- Focus on the individual. One of the best ways to truly understand a differing point of view is to examine it through the eyes of the individual. Strip out the emotion and examine what shaped her. What formed her? What was going on nationally or locally that caused her actions? How did society change because of her? People's misdeeds do not necessarily negate the good they did, but seeing a person as a whole, with flaws, helps to humanize rather than deify them.
- Be aware of word choice. It is, for example, possible to acknowledge the sacrifices of Confederate soldiers and what that sacrifice still means to many southerners without honoring the institution of slavery they were fighting for. A walking tour may not be the avenue to address the complexities of the Civil War, but we can find common ground by remembering the profound loss of life and sacrifice made on both sides. As the dead become what the survivors attribute to them,[2] we can choose to emphasize various aspects of their lives as it suits our agendas.

Collect Information

Once you start to attract audiences to your cemetery, collect contact information. If you have access to a database of contacts, send a survey. Ask what events respondents would be interested in attending. Create simple survey cards to hand out following every event. These survey cards should include the following information:

- Name and contact information. People hesitant to give out phone numbers will be more willing to give out an email address.
- Would you like to join our mailing list?
- Have you ever attended an event in our cemetery?
- Where did you hear about the event?

- What kind of tour or event would you be interested in attending?
- Rate the event. Ask respondents to grade the content of the tour, speaker, appearance of grounds, and refreshments. Use a numeric system to encourage feedback and to quantify results.

Use visitor feedback both to improve the event and to try to discern where your audience is coming from and which outlets are most effective for reaching them. Where are most visitors hearing about you, and where are they coming from? Can you more specifically target a certain market, knowing what types of messages are most likely to resonate?

Bring in "Alternative" Groups

Once a cemetery has an established base of people interested in programming, in order to grow it needs to find ways to bring in "alternative" groups. Laurel Hill established a Young Friends group, the Antemortem Society of Laurel Hill Cemetery, to involve a younger generation. A group of young adults and professionals (ages twenty-one to thirty-five) "working to preserve Laurel Hill and have a great time doing it," the society holds events, such as Cemetery Quizzo, geared toward a younger audience. The goal is not only to attract a different market to the cemetery but also to create a group of young, invested supporters. Laurel Hill also researched its crossover audiences and realized it shared a large number of patrons with theater groups. This led to the adoption of programming in conjunction with the Philadelphia Fringe Festival, which highlights the work of contemporary cutting-edge artists and features works of visual art, dance, and theater. This collaboration has helped Laurel Hill develop a new core group of supporters. Green-Wood Cemetery in Brooklyn, New York, also brings in alternative groups by acting as a performance venue as part of Brooklyn's BEAT Festival, an annual showcase of the borough's performing artists. You can also remix your walking tours to appeal to a target audience by focusing on (or developing) stops that will hold special appeal to the group.

Programming as Marketing

Conducting tours and programming in cemeteries is a form of marketing for both historic and active cemeteries. Active cemeteries (cemeteries still conducting burials and selling burial space) use programming to introduce potential buyers to their site in a nonthreatening way. Many of the rural cemeteries use programming in an effort to combat the misconception that they are "old" and that there's "no room" for new burials. Often, due to the famous names and incredible art found on the site, the public believes these cemeteries are restricted to the wealthy. Programming is a way for the cemetery to be seen as more accessible. In addition, as the neighborhoods around these cemeteries have changed in the 175 years since they were founded, some cemeteries must address perceptions that they are unsafe. Tours and programming are effective ways to address many of these concerns. For organizations such as historical societies or local history museums, cemeteries act as opportunities to complement existing exhibits or programs. Creating walking tours can augment existing programming and provide public appeal for these institutions.

Any historic site must grapple with presenting and interpreting sensitive subjects for the general public. It's important to know your mission and to be able to articulate it to justify your programming. Sometimes it's impossible to know what will offend the public—and what may offend one potential audience may engage and excite another. Negative feedback can be mitigated by being aware of your organization's mission and history and being able to communicate that to the public. Don't be afraid to take chances, but be aware that not everything will work. Never lose sight of the fact that these spaces, while great historical and cultural resources, are also laden with enormous emotional symbols. Don't let that stop you. Cemeteries across the country are bringing in thousands of visitors each year with exciting programming. Visitors are ready to experience a cemetery in a new way.

Notes
1. Levy, Lloyd, and Schreiber, *Great Tours!* 116.
2. Faust, *This Republic of Suffering*, 269.

Conclusion
The Past and the Future

In an address given at the dedication of Mount Auburn Cemetery on September 24, 1831, Supreme Court Justice Joseph Story laid out the purposes for cemeteries beyond disposal of the dead. "They may preach lessons, to which none may refuse to listen, and which all, that live, must hear."[1] He saw many of these lessons being revealed by contrasting the city of the living (Boston) with the city of the dead (the cemetery)—and he noted Boston, in the distance across the Charles River, as "at once the object of our admiration and our love" as it "rears its proud eminences, its graceful mansions, its curling smoke, its crowded haunts of business and pleasure, which speak to the eye, and yet leave a noiseless loneliness on the ear."[2] He was speaking with fondness of the many attractions of the city but noting that these pleasures come at a price. The cemetery could act as a partial antidote, and, for a short time, cemeteries like Mount Auburn helped Americans cope with their changing world.

Nearly two hundred years later, cemeteries across the nation are threatened by decreased revenue and increased maintenance costs. The rise in cremation limits the amount of income from burials. Decades of mismanaged funds have left many cemeteries in financial ruin. In some instances, decades of neglect have created unsafe eyesores. Those who understand the value of these spaces and are concerned with preserving them are increasingly open to alternative approaches. In 2015, the city of Austin, Texas, released a visionary Master Plan to preserve and restore the city's cemeteries. In addition to the historical interpretive value of preserving the burial grounds, this plan also addresses the effects of maintained cemeteries on crime and vandalism along with erosion and the environment. Among the recommendations put forth in the plan is the development of cemetery tours and programming.[3]

Programming is by no means a comprehensive answer to the problems facing America's cemeteries; however, implementing programming can be a beginning step in getting the community reinvested in the welfare of the cemetery. It can be a start toward saving these spaces, and they in turn can be used to help the living. Much like Story's vision for cemeteries in his time, cemeteries can help us cope with our ever-changing world. These spaces we take so much for granted can provide refuge and solace, connect us with our living community, and help us understand our place in the world. The act of preserving them becomes a way to help ourselves.

Notes

1. Bigelow, *A History of Mt. Auburn Cemetery*, 156.
2. Bigelow, *A History of Mt. Auburn Cemetery*, 162.
3. Clark, "Designing for the Dead," http://nextcity.org/features/view/how-to-live-in-the-city-of-the-dead.

Appendix A
State and National Preservation Resources

National Resources
National Park Service
The Olmsted Center for Landscape Preservation
Boston National Historical Park
Charlestown Navy Yard, Quarters C
Boston, MA 02129
Phone: 617-241-6954
http://www.nps.gov/oclp/index.htm

The Association for Gravestone Studies
278 Main Street, Suite 207
Greenfield, MA 01301
http://www.gravestonestudies.org

Chicora Foundation, Inc.
PO Box 8664
Columbia, SC 29202
803-787-6910
http://www.chicora.org/cemetery-preservation.html
Information on cemetery preservation, cemetery documenting, workshops, and publications to order or download.

State Resources
The quality and quantity of resources available vary greatly by state, but the links below can point you to information on your state's laws and resources

for documenting and preserving burial grounds in your state, along with preservation resources.

Alabama
State of Alabama Historic Preservation Office
Alabama Historical Commission
468 South Perry Street/PO Box 300900
Montgomery, Alabama 36130-0900
334-242-3184
http://www.preserveala.org

Alabama's Historic Cemeteries: A Basic Guide to Preservation
http://preserveala.org/pdfs/sites/Alabama's%20Historic%20Cemeteries_A%20Basic%20Guide%20to%20Preservation.pdf

Alabama Cemetery Preservation Alliance
PO Box 3932
Montgomery, AL 36109-0932
http://www.alabama-cemetery-preservation.com/welcome.lasso

Alaska
Alaska Department of Natural Resources
Department of History and Archaeology
550 W. 7th Ave, Suite 1260, Anchorage, AK 99501-3557
907-269-8400
http://dnr.alaska.gov/parks/oha/

The Alaska Association for Historic Preservation
PO Box 102205
Anchorage, AK 99510-2205
907-929-9870
http://www.aahp-online.net/

Arizona
State Historic Preservation Office
Arizona State Parks
1300 W. Washington Street
Phoenix, AZ 85007
602-542-4009
http://azstateparks.com/SHPO/index.html

Griffith, Carol and Michael Sullivan. *Places to Remember: Guidance for Inventorying and Maintaining Historic Cemeteries.* Phoenix: Arizona State Parks, 2012.   http://azstateparks.com/publications/downloads/2012_SHPO_ Cemetery_Etiquette.pdf.

Pioneers' Cemetery Association
PO Box 33192
Phoenix, Arizona 85067
pioneercem@yahoo.com
http://www.azhistcemeteries.org/CemPreservation.htm

Arizona Pioneer and Cemetery Research Project
http://apcrp.org/

Arkansas
Arkansas Historic Preservation Program
1500 Tower Building, 323 Center Street
Little Rock, AR 72201
501-324-9880
An agency of the Department of Arkansas Heritage. http://www.arkansas preservation.com/preservation-services/cemetery-preservation/#register.

Trippe-Dillon, Tammie. *Grave Concerns: A Preservation Manual for Historic Cemeteries in Arkansas.* Preservation Manual, Little Rock: Arkansas Historic Preservation Program, n.d. www.arkansaspreservation.com/_literature_132940/Grave_Concerns.

Arkansas Archaeological Survey
Coordinating Office
2475 N Hatch Ave
Fayetteville AR 72704
479-575-3556
arkarch@uark.edu
http://archeology.uark.edu/learn-discover/cemeteries/

California
California Department of Parks and Recreation
Cultural Resources Division
1416 9th Street
Sacramento, CA 95814

916-653-6995
http://www.parks.ca.gov/?page_id=25397
Contains links to preservation sites

California Historic Cemetery Alliance
http://www.califhistcemeteries.org/

Colorado
History Colorado
Office of Archaeology and Historic Preservation
1200 Broadway
Denver, CO 80203
http://www.historycolorado.org/oahp

Colorado Historic Cemetery Association
info@ColoradoHistoricCemeteries.org
http://coloradohistoriccemeteries.org/

Connecticut
Department of Economic and Community Development
State Historic Preservation Office
One Constitution Plaza, 2nd Floor
Hartford, Connecticut 06103
860-256-2800
http://www.ct.gov/cct/cwp/view.asp?a=3948&q=293806

Connecticut Gravestone Network
http://www.ctgravestones.com/

Delaware
Division of Historical and Cultural Affairs
21 The Green
Dover, DE 19901
302-736-7400
http://history.delaware.gov/preservation/cemeteries.shtml

Preservation Delaware
The New Castle Court House Museum
211 Delaware Street
New Castle, DE 19720

302-322-7100
http://preservationde.org/

Florida
Florida Division of Historical Resources
Bureau of Historic Preservation
R. A. Gray Building
500 South Bronough Street
Tallahassee, FL 32399-0250
850-245-6333
http://dos.myflorida.com/historical/

Florida's Lost and Abandoned Graveyards
http://www.floridagraveyards.org/

Georgia
Georgia Department of Natural Resources
Historic Planning Division

DNR Historic Preservation Division
Jewett Center for Historic Preservation
2610 GA Hwy 155, SW
Stockbridge, GA 30281
770-389-7844
http://georgiashpo.org/historic/cemeteries

Hawaii
State of Hawaii
State Historic Preservation
Kakuhihewa Building
601 Kamokila Blvd., Suite 555
Kapolei, HI 96707
808-692-8015
http://dlnr.hawaii.gov/shpd/

Historic Hawaii Foundation
The Dole Cannery
680 Iwilei Road Dole Office Building Tower, Suite 690
Honolulu, HI 96817
808-523-2900
http://historichawaii.org/

Idaho

State Historic Preservation Office
210 Main Street
Boise, ID 83702
208-334-3847
http://history.idaho.gov/state-historic-preservation-office

Idaho Heritage Trust
PO Box 140617
Boise, Idaho 83714
208-549-1778
http://www.idahoheritage.org/index.html

Illinois

Illinois Department of Natural Resources
Illinois Historic Preservation Agency
Staff Archaeologist
#1 Old State Capitol Plaza
Springfield, Illinois 62701
217-785-1279
https://www.illinois.gov/ihpa/Preserve/Cemetery/Pages/default.aspx

Indiana

Indiana Department of Natural Resources
Division of Historic Preservation and Archaeology
402 West Washington Street
Indianapolis, IN 46204
http://www.in.gov/dnr/historic/3744.htm

Indiana Historical Society
450 West Ohio Street
Indianapolis, IN 46202
317-232-1882
http://www.indianahistory.org/

Indiana Pioneer Cemeteries Restoration Project
http://www.rootsweb.ancestry.com/~inpcrp/

Iowa

Iowa State Historic Preservation Office
State Historical Building

3rd Floor East (Enter the Research Center Doors on Grand Ave.)
600 E Locust St.
Des Moines, IA 50319
http://www.iowahistory.org/historic-preservation/index.html

State Association for the Preservation of Iowa Cemeteries
http://www.rootsweb.ancestry.com/~iasapc/

Kansas
Kansas Historical Society
6425 SW 6th Avenue
Topeka KS 66615
785-272-8681
http://www.kshs.org/

Kentucky
Kentucky Historical Society
100 West Broadway
Frankfort, KY 40601
502-564-1792
http://history.ky.gov/portfolio/cemetery-preservation/

Preservation Kentucky
230 Saint Clair Street
Frankfort, KY 40601
502-871-4570

PO Box 5192
Frankfort, KY 40602
http://www.preservationkentucky.org

Louisiana
Office of Cultural Development
Division of Archaeology
PO Box 44247
Baton Rouge, LA 70804
225-342-8170
http://www.crt.state.la.us/archaeology/

Save Our Cemeteries
501 Basin Street

Suite 3C
New Orleans, LA 70112
504-525-3377
http://www.saveourcemeteries.org/

Maine
Maine Historic Preservation Commission
55 Capitol Street, 65 State House Station
Augusta, Maine 04333-0065
207-287-2132
http://www.state.me.us/mhpc/index.shtml

Maine Cemetery Association
http://mainecemetery.org/

Maine Old Cemetery Association
PO Box 641
Augusta, ME 04332-0641
http://www.moca-me.org/

Maryland
Maryland Historical Trust
Maryland Department of Planning
100 Community Place, Crownsville, MD 21032-2023
410-514-7600
http://mht.maryland.gov/research_cemeteries.shtml

Coalition to Protect Maryland Burial Sites, Inc.
PO Box 1533
Ellicott City, MD 21041-1533
http://www.rootsweb.ancestry.com/~mdcpmbs/coalition01.htm

Massachusetts
Office of Cultural Resources
Department of Conservation and Recreation
251 Causeway Street, Suite 600
Boston MA 02114-2119
617-626-1250
www.mass.gov/dcr

Preservation Massachusetts
Old City Hall
45 School Street
Boston, MA 02108
617-723-3383
http://preservationmass.org/programs/historic-burial-grounds/
Free pdf download, *Preservation Guidelines for Municipally Owned Historic Burial Grounds and Cemeteries*, includes a history of cemetery development, information on preservation guidelines, and case studies. http://www.mass .gov/eea/agencies/dcr/conservation/cultural-resources/publications.html.

Michigan
Michigan State Historic Preservation Office
702 West Kalamazoo Street
Lansing, Michigan 48909
517-373-1630
www.michigan.gov/shpo

Michigan Historic Cemeteries Preservation Guide
http://www.michigan.gov/documents/hal_mhc_shpo_Cemetery_Guide_105082_7.pdf

Minnesota
State Historic Preservation Office
Minnesota Historical Society
345 Kellogg Blvd. W.
St. Paul, MN 55102-1903
Phone: 651-259-3450
mnshpo@mnhs.org
http://www.mnhs.org/shpo/

Preservation Alliance of Minnesota
416 Landmark Center, 75 West 5th Street
Saint Paul, MN 55102
651.293.9047
http://www.mnpreservation.org

Minnesota Association of Cemeteries
3600 Hennepin Avenue
Minneapolis, MN 55408

612-822-2171
fax: 612-822-0575
info@mncemeteries.org

Mississippi

Mississippi Department of Archives and History
1596 Glenn Swetman Street
Biloxi, MS 39530
info@mdah.state.ms.us
601-576-6850

Preservation in Mississippi
http://misspreservation.com/

Missouri
State Historic Preservation Office

PO Box 176
Jefferson City, MO 65102
800-361-4827
573-751-7858
http://dnr.mo.gov/shpo/

Missouri Preservation
320 First Street
Boonville, MO 65233
660-882-5946
http://www.preservemo.org/

Montana

Montana Historic State Preservation Office
1410 Eighth Avenue
Helena, MT 59620
406-444-7715
mtshpo@mt.gov
https://mhs.mt.gov/Shpo

Montana Preservation Alliance
120 Reeder's Alley
Helena, MT 59601
406-457-2822

http://www.preservemontana.org/
info@preservemontana.org

Nebraska
Nebraska State Historical Society
Nebraska State Historic Preservation Office
PO Box 82554
1500 R Street
Lincoln, NE 68501
http://nebraskahistory.org

Nebraska State Historical Society
Cemetery Registry
PO Box 82554
Lincoln, NE 68501-2554
402-471-4786
nshs.cemetery@nebraska.gov

Nevada
Nevada State Historic Preservation Office
901 S. Stewart Street, Suite 5004
Carson City, NV 89701
775-684-3448
shpo-info@shpo.nv.gov
http://shpo.nv.gov/

New Hampshire
New Hampshire Department of Cultural Resources
20 Park Street
Concord, NH 03301
603-271-2392
http://www.nh.gov/nhculture/index.htm

New Hampshire Preservation Alliance
7 Eagle Square
PO Box 268
Concord, NH 03302-0268
603-224-2281
http://www.nhpreservation.org/

New Hampshire Old Graveyard Association
http://www.nhoga.com
webmaster@nhoga.com

New Hampshire Cemetery Association
107 Amherst St.
Nashua, NH 03064
603-594-3327
http://www.nhcemetery.org

New Jersey
New Jersey Department of Environmental Protection
Historic Preservation Office
501 East State Street
Plaza Building 5
4th Floor
Mailing Address: Mail Code 501-04B
State of New Jersey
Department of Environmental Protection
Historic Preservation Office
PO Box 420
Trenton, NJ 08625-0420
609-984-0176
http://www.nj.gov/dep/hpo/

Preservation New Jersey
PO Box 7815
West Trenton, NJ 08628
609-392-6409
info@preservationnj.org
http://www.preservationnj.org/site/ExpEng/

State of New Jersey
New Jersey Historic Trust
http://www.njht.org/dca/njht/

New Jersey Cemetery Association
PMB 365
1253 Springfield Ave
New Providence, NJ 07974

973-566-6522
ExecutiveDirector@njcaonline.org
http://www.njcaonline.org/

New Mexico
New Mexico Historic Preservation Division
Department of Cultural Affairs
Bataan Memorial Building
407 Galisteo Street, Suite 236
Santa Fe, NM 87501
505-827-6320
http://www.nmhistoricpreservation.org/

New York
Department of State
Division of Cemeteries
Department of State, Albany Location:
One Commerce Plaza, 99 Washington Ave
Albany, NY 12231-0001
518-474-6226
http://www.dos.ny.gov/cmty/index.html

New York State Historic Preservation Office
Peebles Island Resource Center
PO Box 189
Waterford, NY 12188-0189
518-237-8643
http://nysparks.com/historic-preservation/

New York Historic Cemetery Preservation Society, Inc.
PO Box 15
Little Falls, NY 13365
315-663-8962
http://www.nyhcps.org/

North Carolina
North Carolina State Historic Preservation Office
109 E. Jones St.
Raleigh NC 27601
Mailing Address: 4617 Mail Service Center

Raleigh, NC 27699-4617
919-807-6570
http://www.hpo.ncdcr.gov/links.htm

North Carolina Office of State Archaeology
http://www.arch.dcr.state.nc.us/ncarch/reporting/cemetery.htm

North Carolina Cemetery Survey Project
North Carolina Office of Archives & History
4614 Mail Service Center
Raleigh, NC 27699-4614

North Dakota
State Historical Society of North Dakota
State Historic Preservation Office
612 E Boulevard Ave
Bismarck, ND 58505
701-328-2672
http://history.nd.gov/hp/

Preservation North Dakota
PND, 911 N 9th Street, PO Box 3096
Bismarck, ND 58502
701-226-5359
info@prairieplaces.org
http://www.preservationnorthdakota.org/

Ohio
Ohio History Center
800 E. 17th Ave.
Columbus, OH 43211
614-297-2300
https://www.ohiohistory.org/

Ohio Genealogical Society
611 State Route 97 West
Bellville, OH 44813-8813
https://www.ogs.org/research/cemeteries.php

Ohio Cemetery Preservation Society
http://www.rootsweb.ancestry.com/~ohcps/

Oklahoma
Oklahoma Historical Society
Oklahoma History Center
800 Nazih Zuhdi Drive
Oklahoma City, OK 73105
405-521-2491
http://www.okhistory.org/shpo/shpom.htm

Preservation Oklahoma, Inc.
The Henry Overholser Mansion
Carriage House
405 NW 15th Street
Oklahoma City, OK 73103
405-525-5325
http://www.preservationok.org/home.html

Oregon
Oregon Commission on Historic Cemeteries
Historic Cemeteries Program, OPRD
725 Summer St. NE, Suite C
Salem, OR 97301
http://www.oregon.gov/oprd/HCD/OCHC/Pages/index.aspx

Oregon Historic Cemeteries Association
PO Box 15251
Portland, OR 97293
http://www.oregoncemeteries.org/Home

Pennsylvania
Pennsylvania Historical and Museum Commission
Bureau for Historic Preservation
Commonwealth Keystone Building
400 North Street
Harrisburg, PA 17120
717-783-8946
http://www.portal.state.pa.us/portal/server.pt/community/cemetery_re-
cordation_and_preservation/1875

Rhode Island
Rhode Island Historical Preservation & Heritage Commission
Old State House

150 Benefit Street
Providence, RI 02903
401-222-2678
http://www.preservation.ri.gov/

Rhode Island Historical Cemetery Commission
PO Box 8993
Warwick, RI 02888
401-467-8142
http://www.rihistoriccemeteries.org/

South Carolina
South Carolina Department of Archives and History
State Historic Preservation Office
8301 Parklane Road
Columbia, SC 29223
803-896-6196
http://shpo.sc.gov/tech/Pages/Cemeteries.aspx

South Carolina's Historic Cemeteries: A Preservation Handbook. Free pdf download featuring a historical overview of South Carolina's cemeteries and laws.
http://shpo.sc.gov/pubs/Documents/cemeterypres.pdf.

South Dakota
State Historic Preservation Office
900 Governors Dr.
Pierre, SD 57501
605-773-3458
http://history.sd.gov/Preservation/

Preserve South Dakota
PO Box 743
Mitchell, SD 57301
http://preservesd.org/

Tennessee
Tennessee Historical Commission
312 Rosa L. Parks Ave
Nashville, TN 37243
888-891-8332
http://www.tn.gov/environment/section/tennessee-historical-commission

Tennessee Division of Archaeology
1216 Foster Avenue
Cole Building #3
Nashville, TN 37243

Tennessee Preservation Trust
PO Box 24373
Nashville, TN 37202
615-963-1255
http://www.tennesseepreservationtrust.org/

Texas
Texas Historical Commission
PO Box 12276
Austin, TX 78711-2276
512-463-5853
http://www.thc.state.tx.us/
http://www.thc.state.tx.us/preserve/projects-and-programs/cemetery-preservation

Free pdf download *Preserving Historic Cemeteries: Texas Preservation Guidelines*, http://www.thc.state.tx.us/public/upload/publications/preserving-historic-cemeteries.pdf.

Preservation Texas
PO Box 12832
Austin, TX 78711
512.472.0102
http://www.preservationtexas.org/endangered/historic-texas-cemeteries/

Utah
Utah Division of State History
300 S. Rio Grande Street (450 West)
Salt Lake City, UT 84101
801-245-7225
http://heritage.utah.gov/history/cemeteries

Utah Heritage Foundation
Memorial House in Memory Grove Park
375 N. Canyon Rd.
Salt Lake City, Utah 84103

801-533-0858
http://www.utahheritagefoundation.org/

Vermont
Vermont Division for Historic Preservation
5696 Monument Hill Road
Bomoseen, VT 05732
(802) 273-2282
http://accd.vermont.gov/strong_communities/preservation/

Vermont Cemetery Association
39 Main Street
Montpelier, VT 05602
802-223-5352
http://www.vermontcemeteryassociation.org/

Vermont Old Cemetery Association
http://www.voca58.org/index.html

Vermont Cemetery Restoration and Preservation
http://www.underbrush.org/

Virginia
Virginia Department of Historic Resources
2801 Kensington Avenue
Richmond, VA 23221
(804) 482-6446
http://www.dhr.virginia.gov

Department of Historic Resources
Historic Cemeteries in Virginia
http://dhrcemeteries.blogspot.com/

Preservation Virginia
204 West Franklin Street
Richmond, VA 23220-5012
804-648-1889
info@preservationvirginia.org
http://preservationvirginia.org

Washington
Department of Archaeology and Historic Preservation
1110 S. Capitol Way, Suite 30
Olympia, WA 98501
360-586-3065
Mailing Address: PO Box 48343
Olympia, WA 98504-8343
http://www.dahp.wa.gov/cemetery-program

Wisconsin
Wisconsin Historical Society
816 State Street
Madison, WI 53706
http://www.wisconsinhistory.org

Wisconsin Cemetery and Cremation Association
http://www.wiscemeteries.org/

West Virginia
West Virginia Division of Culture and Industry
West Virginia State Historic Preservation Office
1900 Kanawha Blvd E
Charleston, WV 25305
304-558-0220
http://www.wvculture.org/shpo/cemeteries.html

West Virginia Cemetery Preservation Association, Inc.
PO Box 131
Leon, WV 25123
http://wvcpaweb.org/

Wyoming
Wyoming State Historic Preservation Office
Barrett Building—3rd Floor
2301 Central Avenue
Cheyenne, WY 82002
307-777-7697
http://wyoshpo.state.wy.us/

Appendix B
Recommended Reading

Cemetery History

Eggener, Keith. *Cemeteries*. New York: W. W. Norton & Company, 2010.

Linden, Blanche M. G. *Silent City on a Hill: Picturesque Landscapes of Memory and Boston's Mount Auburn Cemetery*. Amherst and Boston: University of Massachusetts Press, 2007.

McDowell, Peggy, and Richard E. Meyer. *The Revival Styles in American Memorial Art*. Bowling Green: Bowling Green State University Popular Press, 1994.

Sloane, David Charles. *The Last Great Necessity: Cemeteries in American History*. Baltimore: Johns Hopkins University Press, 1991.

Yalom, Marilyn. *The American Resting Place: Four Hundred Years of History through Our Cemeteries and Burial Grounds*. Boston: Houghton Mifflin Company, 2008.

Cemetery Symbolism and Material Culture

Keister, Douglas. *Stories in Stone: A Field Guide to Cemetery Symbolism and Iconography*. Salt Lake City: Gibbs Smith, 2004.

Meyer, Richard E., ed. *Cemeteries & Gravemarkers: Voices of American Culture*. Logan: Utah State University Press, 1992.

Cemetery Preservation and Documentation

Griffith, Carol, and Michael Sullivan. *Places to Remember: Guidance for Inventorying and Maintaining Historic Cemeteries*. Phoenix: Arizona State Parks, 2012.

King, Greg G., and Susan Kosky, Kathleen Glynn, and Gladys Saborio. *Michigan Historic Cemeteries Preservation Guide*. Canton: Michigan State Historic Preservation Office, 2004.

Potter, Elisabeth Walton, and Beth M. Boland. "Guidelines for Evaluating and Registering Cemeteries and Burial Places." *National Register Bulletin 41*. Washington, DC: U.S. Department of the Interior, National Park Service, 1992.

Strangstad, Lynette. *A Graveyard Preservation Primer*. Second Edition. Lanham: AltaMira Press, 2013.

Trippe-Dillon, Tammie. *Grave Concerns: A Preservation Manual for Historic Cemeteries in Arkansas*. Preservation Manual, Little Rock: Arkansas Historic Preservation Program, n.d.

Conducting Research

Carmack, Sharon DeBartolo. *Your Guide to Cemetery Research*. Cincinnati: Betterway Books, 2002.

Bibliography

American Trails. *American Trails*. 2014. http://www.americantrails.org/national recreationtrails (accessed December 8, 2014).

Bender, Thomas. "The 'Rural' Cemetery Movement: Urban Travail and the Appeal of Nature." *New England Quarterly* 47, no. 2 (1974): 196–211.

Bigelow, Jacob. *A History of Mt. Auburn Cemetery*. Cambridge: Applewood Books, 1988.

Bronner, Simon J. *American Material Culture and Folklife: A Prologue and Dialogue*. Logan: Utah State University Press, 1992.

Carmack, Sharon DeBartolo. *Your Guide to Cemetery Research*. Cincinnati: Betterway Books, 2002.

Carver, Erin. *Birding in the United States: A Demographic and Economic Analysis*. Arlington: U.S. Fish and Wildlife Service, 2013.

Ciregna, Elise Madeline. "Museum in the Garden: Mount Auburn Cemetery and American Sculpture, 1840–1860." *Markers XX1* (2004): 100–147.

Clark, Anna. "Designing for the Dead: The Perfect City Cemetery." *Next City*, March 2, 2015. http://nextcity.org/features/view/how-to-live-in-the-city-of-the-dead (accessed April 10, 2015).

Cook, Jr., Zebedee. "An Address, Pronounced Before the Massachusetts Horticultural Society in Commemoration of its Second Annual Festival." Boston: Isaac R. Butts, 1830.

Cremation Association of North America. *Cremation Association of North America Industry Statistics*. 2015. http://www.cremationassociation.org/?page=Industry Statistics (accessed August 30, 2015).

Downing, A. J. *Rural Essays*. New York: Leavitt & Allen, 1860.

Downing, Elliot R., ed. *The Nature-Study Review* (Comstock Publishing Company) 11, no. 6 (September 1915).

Edgette, J. Joseph. "The Epitaph and Personality Revelation." In *Cemeteries & Gravemarkers: Voices of American Culture*, edited by Richard E. Meyer, 87–102. Logan: Utah University Press, 1992.

Eggener, Keith. *Cemeteries*. New York: W. W. Norton & Company, 2010.

Faust, Drew Gilpin. *This Republic of Suffering: Death and the American Civil War*. New York: Vintage Books, 2008.

Fenza, Paula J. "Communities of the Dead: Tombstones as a Reflection of Social Organization." Edited by Theodore Chase. *Markers: Journal of the Association for Gravestone Studies* (University Press of America) VI (1989): 137–58.

Flagg, Wilson. *Mount Auburn: Its Scenes, Its Beauties and Its Lessons*. Cambridge: J. Munroe and Company, 1861.

Foster, Gary S., and Richard L. Hummel. "The Adkins-Woodson Cemetery: A Sociological Examination of Cemeteries as Communities." *Markers* (Association for Gravestone Studies) 12 (1995): 93–117.

Friends of Mount Auburn. "Ornithologists and Benefactors of Birds at Mount Auburn." n.d. http://issuu.com/friendsofmountauburn/docs/ornithologists_04-2013_kmr_final.

Griffith, Carol, and Michael Sullivan. *Places to Remember: Guidance for Inventorying and Maintaining Historic Cemeteries*. Phoenix: Arizona State Parks, 2012.

Harnik, Peter. *Urban Green: Innovative Parks for Resurgent Cities*. Washington: Island Press, 2010.

Keister, Douglas. *Stories in Stone: A Field Guide to Cemetery Symbolism and Iconography*. Salt Lake City: Gibbs Smith, 2004.

King, Greg G., and Susan Kosky, Kathleen Glynn, and Gladys Saborio. *Michigan Historic Cemeteries Preservation Guide*. Canton: Michigan State Historic Preservation Office, 2004.

Laderman, Gary. *The Sacred Remains: American Attitudes Toward Death, 1799–1883*. New Haven: Yale University Press, 1996.

Laurel Hill Cemetery. "Meeting of the Managers, January 19th 1844." Philadelphia: Laurel Hill Cemetery, January 19, 1844.

Levy, Barbara Abramoff, Sandra Mackenzie Lloyd, and Susan Porter Schreiber. *Great Tours! Thematic Tours and Guide Training for Historic Sites*. Walnut Creek: AltaMira Press, 2001.

Linden, Blanche M. G. *Silent City on a Hill: Picturesque Landscapes of Memory and Boston's Mount Auburn Cemetery*. Amherst and Boston: University of Massachusetts Press, 2007.

Linden-Ward, Blanche. "Strange but Genteel Pleasure Grounds: Tourist and Leisure Uses of Nineteenth-Century Rural Cemeteries." In *Cemeteries & Gravemarkers: Voices of American Culture*, edited by Richard E. Meyer, 293–328. Logan: Utah State University Press, 1992.

Loving, Susan. "Heel; Sit; Stay; Roll Over—and Don't Walk on the Graves." *ICCFA Magazine*, December 2014, 14–19.

McDannell, Colleen. *Material Christianity: Religion and Material Culture in America.* New Haven: Yale University Press, 1995.

McDowell, Peggy, and Richard E. Meyer. *The Revival Styles in American Memorial Art.* Bowling Green: Bowling Green State University Popular Press, 1994.

McGahee, Susan H., and Mary W. Edmonds. *South Carolina's Historic Cemeteries: A Preservation Handbook.* South Carolina Department of Archives and History, 1997.

Meyer, Richard E., ed. *Cemeteries & Gravemarkers: Voices of American Culture.* Logan: Utah State University Press, 1992.

National Humane Review. "The Largest Cemetery Bird Sanctuary in America." *National Humane Review,* July 1916, 152.

Pearson, T. Gilbert. *The Bird Study Book.* Garden City: Doubleday, Page & Company, 1919.

Perazzo, Peggy B., and George Perazzo. *Quarries and Beyond.* n.d. http://quarries andbeyond.org/index.html (accessed November 2, 2015).

Potter, Elisabeth Walton, and Beth M. Boland. "Guidelines for Evaluating and Registering Cemeteries and Burial Places." *National Register Bulletin 41.* Washington, DC: U.S. Department of the Interior, National Park Service, 1992.

Richman, Jeffrey I. *Brooklyn's Green-Wood Cemetery: New York's Buried Treasure.* Brooklyn: Green-Wood Cemetery, 1998.

Sachs, Aaron. *Arcadian America: The Death and Life of an Environmental Tradition.* New Haven: Yale University Press, 2013.

Sloane, David Charles. *The Last Great Necessity: Cemeteries in American History.* Baltimore: Johns Hopkins University Press, 1991.

Smith, R. A. *Smith's Illustrated Guide to and Through Laurel Hill Cemetery.* Philadelphia: Willis P. Hazard, 1852.

Strangstad, Lynette. *A Graveyard Preservation Primer.* Second Edition. Lanham: AltaMira Press, 2013.

Tiffany Glass and Decorating Company. "Out-of-Door Memorials: Mausoleums, Tombs, Headstones, and All Forms of Mortuary Monuments." New York: Tiffany Glass and Decorating Company, 1898.

Trippe-Dillon, Tammie. *Grave Concerns: A Preservation Manual for Historic Cemeteries in Arkansas.* Preservation Manual, Little Rock: Arkansas Historic Preservation Program, n.d.

Woodlawn Cemetery and Arboretum. *Birds of Woodlawn.* 2012. http://www .historic-woodlawn.com/birds.html (accessed January 15, 2015).

Yalom, Marilyn. *The American Resting Place: Four Hundred Years of History through Our Cemeteries and Burial Grounds.* Boston: Houghton Mifflin Company, 2008.

Index

natural features inventories for,
36–37
New Haven Connecticut Bird Club,
"The Big Sit!" of, 89
North Carolina Bluebird Society, 90
North Carolina Blue Bird Trail, 68
Notman, John, 84

Oakland Cemetery, Atlanta, Georgia,
15, 79; as death café host, 105–6;
Gone with the Wind Trail of, 78;
Halloween tours in, *117*; Sunday
picnics in, 93–94
Oak Openings Loop, Lake Erie
Birding Trail, 90
Oakwood Cemetery, North Carolina:
The Birds & The Bees of
Oakwood Cemetery program, 68,
90; evening open houses of, 115;
NC Science Festival case study of,
63–68, *67*
Ocmulgee Heritage Trail, 77, 78
"ofrenda" (altar of remembrance), 109
Old City Cemetery, Lynchburg,
Virginia, 85
"101 Tour," 38–39, 48, 114

*Park and Cemetery and Landscape
Gardening* (industry publication), 86
Pearson, T. Gilbert, 86
Pennsylvania Railroad, 76, 104
performing arts programming: concerts
and movie nights in, 92–93;
connecting with cemetery in, 92;
theatre groups and dance troupes
in, 92
Philadelphia Fringe Festival, 119
photography programming, 90; night
session suggestions for, 91
picnic programming, 93–94
politicalgraveyard.com, 23
Portland Trails website, 75
private family mausoleum, 26

quarriesandbeyond.org, 36

recreation programming: cemetery
space guides for, 74; competitive
races and fun runs as, 78–80;
different rules in, 72–73; dogs and
cemeteries in, 80–83; physical
activities list for, 75; questions to
answer in, 94; respectfulness in,
73; visual backdrop in, 74; walking
clubs as, 75; walking trails as,
75–78
religious or ethnic cemeteries, 2–3
remembrance programming:
anniversaries of tragic events as,
100–101; annual memorial service
in, 100; Easter as, 100; holidays
in, 99; Jewish tradition of, 99;
remembering dead in, 99–100; tips
on, 106; wreath-laying ceremony
as, 100
Revolutionary War, 10, 101
Riverside Cemetery, Macon, Georgia,
90; Ocmulgee Heritage Trail link
with, 77, 78
Riverside Cemetery Conservancy, 78
Rosehill Cemetery, Chicago, 79
rural cemeteries, 9; for burial
needs of growing population,
10; as first municipal parks,
2, 13, 71–72; first tribute or
commemorative memorials in, 98;
as model for book, 3; as places for
contemplation, 97, 99; process of
death and family changes by, 13; as
providing cultural enrichment, 10;
as public garden, 84; Revolutionary
War regarding, 10; transition from
church-controlled burial grounds
to, 98–99; view of nature in, 97–98

Schuylkill Division Pennsylvania
Railroad line, 76

About the Author

Rachel Wolgemuth has a background in American studies. Her graduate research focused on folklore and material culture with an emphasis on American cemeteries, specifically the rural cemetery movement and pet cemeteries. Since joining West Laurel Hill Cemetery in 2005, she has worked in various administrative capacities and has helped to create and develop numerous events and programs at West Laurel Hill.